FINDING YOUR RHYTHM

FINDING YOUR RHYTHM

Time Management for the Creative Mind

Pedro "sP" Polanco

Copyright © 2024 sP Polanco
All rights reserved. No portion of this book may be reproduced in any form without written permission from the publisher or author, except as permitted by U.S. copyright law.

www.sPPolanco.com

Designations used by companies to distinguish their products are often claimed as trademarks. All brand names and product names used in this book are trade names, service marks, trademarks or registered trademarks of their respective owners. The author and publisher are not associated with any product or vendor mentioned in this book unless specified.

This publication is designed to provide accurate and authoritative information regarding the subject matter covered. It is sold with the understanding that neither the author nor the publisher is engaged in rendering legal, investment, accounting or other professional services. While the publisher and author have used their best efforts in preparing this book, they make no representations or warranties with respect to the accuracy or completeness of the contents of this book and specifically disclaim any implied warranties of merchantability or fitness for a particular purpose. No warranty may be created or extended by sales representatives or written sales materials. The advice and strategies contained herein may not be suitable for your situation. You should consult with a professional when appropriate. Neither the publisher nor the author shall be liable for any loss of profit or any other commercial damages, including but not limited to special, incidental, consequential, personal, or other damages.

ISBN: 9798332697289 (Paperback)
ISBN: 9798333009050 (Hardcover)

For those that dream while still awake.

Contents

Foreword	XI
The Importance of Time Management for Creatives	**1**
What is Time Management?	2
"But time management ruins my creativity."	4
Personal and Professional Benefits of Time Management	5
"But... how and where do I even begin?"	6
Maximize Your Time and Get Things Done	**9**
Time management techniques to increase productivity	11
Chapter 2 Summary	27
Nurturing Creativity While Owning Your Time	**31**
Combining time management and creative work.	35

Chapter Summary: 39

SETTING, PRIORITIZING AND CRUSHING YOUR GOALS   41

Prioritization tools and techniques 44
Chapter Summary 54

FROM PLANNING TO EXECUTION   57

Understanding the Creative Journey 58
Define Clear Goals 59
Create a Realistic Schedule 62
Build Your Support System 66
Consistency Over Perfection 68
Track Progress and Celebrate Milestones 69
Chapter Summary 70

WORKING WITH A TEAM   73

Team building and collaboration 74
Techniques for effective communication and delegation 75
Real-life examples of successful collaboration in the music industry 77
How to manage team members' time effectively 79

OVERCOMING PROCRASTINATION AND DISTRACTIONS   83

Mindset and Attitude 84

Overcoming procrastination and distractions	86
Mindfulness and self-awareness	88
Chapter 7 Summary	95

THE POWER OF INTENTIONAL LIVING — **97**

Intentional living and setting priorities	98
Strategies for avoiding burnout	99
How to create a fulfilling and balanced life	108

CONCLUSION — **111**

AUTHOR BIO — **115**

Foreword

Time— it's the pulse of our universe, a never-ending rhythm that orchestrates our very existence. We feel its significance in the smallest of rituals, from the anticipation of a New Year countdown to the ticking of the seconds of a watch on our wrist. Yet, time waits for no one. Each moment, once passed, is lost forever. To truly unlock the magic of time, we must consciously acknowledge it and practice the art of harnessing it. As a 4-time Latin Grammy-nominated, multi-platinum producer and ASCAP award-winning composer with over two decades in the music industry, I've experienced firsthand the critical role of effective time management in balancing my creativity, productivity, and personal life.

My name is sP Polanco. This book represents the lessons I've learned throughout my journey, both as an independent creative and an executive in one of the music industry's major record labels. I've navigated the complexities of managing multiple projects, meeting tight deadlines, and maintaining creative momentum, all while ensuring my personal life didn't fall by the wayside.

While I don't claim to be an expert in time management, my experiences have led me to deeply explore and experiment with various methods. It's important to note that plenty of resources are written from a more scientific and studied perspective. My aim is to share advice based on what I've personally encountered and found effective. This book is about sharing what has worked for me in the hope that these insights can benefit your creative journey.

My approach isn't about squeezing more tasks into an already packed day. It's about making space for creativity, developing a mindset focused on achieving goals and enhancing the overall quality of life. It's about applying time management principles tailored explicitly for the unique challenges and rhythms of the creative process.

We'll start with the fundamentals: understanding the core principles of time management, its applicability in the creative industry, and dispelling common misconceptions holding you back. Then, we'll go into specific strategies and tools designed to boost your productivity without stifling your creativity.

No journey is without its obstacles. In the creative field, procrastination, distractions, and burnout are common. We'll address these issues with practical, actionable advice, helping you navigate these challenges effectively.

By the end of this book, you'll have a deeper understanding of the significance of time management in your creative pursuits. Whether you're a seasoned professional or just starting out, the insights and strategies shared here will empower you to enhance your career, achieve your goals, and lead a balanced, fulfilling life.

1

THE IMPORTANCE OF TIME MANAGEMENT FOR CREATIVES

In the 20 years I've been a record producer, composer, and, more recently, a music executive, I have seen firsthand the power of effective time management. But it wasn't always easy for me. Early in my career, I struggled to juggle the different aspects of being a professional creative, from writing and recording to promoting and touring. I was overwhelmed and frustrated by the never-ending to-do list, often feeling like I needed more time in the day to complete everything.

Through years of trial and error, I learned the importance of time management and its role in achieving success in music. Effective time management is not just about working harder or faster; it's about working smarter and maximizing your available time and resources.

This chapter will explore the fundamentals of time management, including its definition and importance in the creative field. We'll also explore some common myths and misconceptions and debunk them with real-life examples.

One of the most significant benefits of effective time management is its impact on your personal and professional life. By managing your time more efficiently, you can free up more time for leisure, hobbies, and spending time with loved ones. You'll also be able to focus more on your creative work, leading to higher-quality output and greater satisfaction in your career.

We'll explore various time management techniques and strategies to achieve these benefits. We'll cover everything from setting goals and priorities to using tools like calendars and digital apps. We'll also discuss the importance of self-awareness and identifying your productivity style to determine which techniques work best for you.

What is Time Management?

Time management, simply put, is organizing and prioritizing time effectively to achieve your goals. Time management is essential to success in the constantly evolving music industry. Everyone in this business, from artists and producers to managers and executives, faces tight schedules, demanding deadlines, and high-pressure situations. Still, the only way to meet these challenges and achieve their goals with balance, purpose, and fulfillment is to take control of their time.

The music industry is a complex and multifaceted business that requires constant attention and effort. It involves not only creative work like songwriting, composing, and producing but also strategic planning, marketing, and networking. Without adequate time management, one can quickly become overwhelmed and unable to meet deadlines, accomplish tasks, or pursue more significant opportunities. By mastering time management techniques, one can increase productivity, creativity, and chances for overall success.

Effective time management in the creative realm also involves prioritizing tasks and responsibilities. With so many demands on their time, professionals must be able to distinguish between urgent and essential tasks and allocate their time accordingly. Prioritization helps you to focus on the most critical and meaningful activities and avoid distractions and time-wasting tasks. With proper prioritization, you can achieve your goals efficiently and effectively.

Time management also plays a crucial role in managing stress and avoiding burnout. A career in arts can be stressful, with extended hours, tight deadlines, and intense pressure. Without adequate time management, you can quickly become overwhelmed and experience physical, mental, and emotional exhaustion. By prioritizing tasks, setting boundaries, and practicing self-care, you will soon find that you can manage your stress levels and maintain a healthy work-life balance.

In summary, time management is an essential skill to achieve any level of success. It allows you to manage your time effectively, prioritize tasks, manage stress, and achieve your goals with balance and fulfillment.

"But Time Management Ruins My Creativity."

As much as time management is essential to any career, there are numerous myths and misconceptions surrounding it, particularly in the creative fields. One of the biggest myths is that time management is only about working non-stop and cramming as many tasks as possible into a single day. In reality, efficiency is about working smarter, not harder. Effective time management is about optimizing your time and resources to hit your goals while allowing flexibility and those necessary moments to unwind instead of merely extending your working hours.

Another widespread fallacy is equating busyness with productivity. It's easy to feel accomplished just by being busy, but that doesn't necessarily equate to effectiveness. Being busy without purpose can quickly lead to burnout and deplete your creative energy. It's crucial to be purposeful with your time, understanding how each hour contributes to the bigger picture of your goals. As we progress through this book, we'll explore how to distinguish genuine productivity from mere busy work and set priorities accordingly.

There's also a misconception that time management is rigid, leaving no room for spontaneity or creativity. In fact, effective time management can create more space for creative freedom. When your mind is not weighed down by unmanaged tasks and a never-ending to-do list, it is free to focus on the present moment, capture inspiration, and tap into your inner self. In Chapter 3, we'll explore how mindfulness and structured time can ignite creative sparks, sharing techniques that have helped me merge discipline with creativity.

Also, there's this idea that time management is a one-size-fits-all solution. Not true. It's about finding what works for you and adapting tools and strategies to your unique circumstances and rhythm.

Lastly, it's a myth that time management is only for those in high-pressure roles like CEOs. Truth is, effective time management is vital for anyone looking to maximize their time and achieve their goals, regardless of their career stage or field. It's a tool to reduce stress, enhance productivity, and balance work and life harmoniously. Whether it's about managing your professional projects, an exercise routine, or even your weekend plans, thoughtfully managing your time can profoundly improve your overall quality of life.

Personal and Professional Benefits of Time Management

Practicing time management isn't just about excelling at work; it's a transformative skill that equally enriches your personal life. Getting a grip on your time is like finding the perfect harmony between your career aspirations and the personal moments that bring joy and relaxation.

Productivity Unleashed: By effectively managing time, you turn each day into a well-orchestrated symphony of productivity. Tasks get your full attention, leading to faster completion and work of the highest caliber. This efficiency can fast-track your career goals, setting the stage for more tremendous success.

Stress, Meet Your Conqueror: The beauty of a well-managed schedule is its power to dissolve stress. With your tasks and responsibilities neatly lined up, the overwhelming waves of anxiety recede. You carve out time for self-care, dodging burnout, and nurturing those personal relationships that make life worth living.

A Canvas for Creativity: Structured time might seem counterintuitive to creativity, but it's quite the opposite. With a clear plan in place, your mind is free to wander in the realms of creativity. Dedicating specific hours to creative pursuits can lead to groundbreaking ideas and innovations.

Decisions Made Smarter: Clarity in your priorities and deadlines equips you with the insight to make sound decisions. When your focus is razor-sharp, distractions lose their power, guiding you towards choices that resonate with your goals.

In essence, mastering time management is about painting a bigger picture, one where productivity, peace of mind, creativity, and wise decision-making coexist. It's about shaping a life where each tick of the clock brings you closer to your personal and professional zeniths.

"BUT... HOW AND WHERE DO I EVEN BEGIN?"

There are many time management techniques and strategies, each with its own strengths and weaknesses. From the

Pomodoro technique to the Eisenhower matrix, there are plenty of tools and methods to choose from.

However, it's important to remember that not all techniques will work for everyone. Some may succeed with time blocking and scheduling, while others prefer a more fluid approach. Experimenting with different techniques and finding the ones that work best for your specific needs and preferences is essential.

Moreover, what works for you now may not necessarily work for you in the future. As your responsibilities and priorities change, so may the techniques you find most compelling. For example, batching similar tasks together may be helpful in a project that requires a lot of repetition but may be adequate for a more complex project that requires greater creativity.

Despite these variations, there are some standard techniques that many successful individuals use to manage their time effectively. These include:

1. **Prioritization**: Involves identifying the most critical tasks and allocating time and resources accordingly.
2. **Time blocking:** Setting aside specific time blocks for different tasks or types of work can help increase focus and reduce distractions.
3. **Goal setting:** This involves setting specific and measurable goals and breaking them down into smaller, achievable steps.
4. **Delegation:** Assigning tasks to others with the skills and resources to complete them effectively. In essence,

it frees up more time to do things that are higher on your priority list.
5. **Automation:** This involves using technology or other tools to automate repetitive tasks, which can save time and increase efficiency.

Additionally, it's worth exploring new time management techniques and constantly emerging tools. Technology, for example, has brought a wealth of new tools that can help with time management, such as apps, online calendars, productivity software, and even artificial intelligence. It's worth experimenting with these tools to find the best ones.

In the following chapters, we will dive deeper into some of these tools and techniques and explore how they can be practically applied.

2

MAXIMIZE YOUR TIME AND GET THINGS DONE

In the early 2000s, as I began making waves in the music industry, I faced a reality that many creatives encounter: the scarcity of time. My initial approach was simple – immerse myself in the studio and let creativity flow. But as my name grew in the industry, so did the complexities of managing my time. The idea of juggling multiple projects and strict deadlines quickly transformed from a distant thought to an everyday struggle.

This period was a real test of my time management skills. I constantly started new projects before finishing existing ones, leading to a never-ending catch-up cycle. My productivity was impacted, sleep became a luxury, and my personal life began to feel like an afterthought. Success was there, but it was overshadowed by a constant feeling overwhelmed.

The challenges I faced were multifaceted. The most pressing issue was managing multiple projects, which seemed essential for success in the music industry. I thought I could handle everything – but in reality, I was spreading myself too thin. The lack of clear priorities meant I was always busy but not necessarily effective.

Distractions and interruptions were relentless. My phone was a constant source of disruption, my inbox was always full, and my schedule was crammed with commitments. Without a solid plan, I felt like I was always running out of time, struggling to stay focused and productive.

Creative blockages presented another hurdle. Creativity, the lifeblood of my work, started to feel forced and elusive. Staring at a blank screen or an empty studio became a typical scenario, signaling a well of ideas that had temporarily dried up.

But perhaps the most significant challenge was burnout. The music industry often glorifies long hours and constant work, but this comes at a cost. I sacrificed my well-being for my career, leading to diminished energy and motivation.

Reflecting on this period, I realize that a lack of strategic planning was at the heart of these challenges. I was so caught up in day-to-day tasks that I lost sight of the bigger picture. Without a clear vision and a structured approach to achieve it, I found myself constantly reacting to immediate demands, unable to manage my time and energy effectively.

Time Management Techniques to Increase Productivity

In the previous chapter, I introduced some common time management, but let's dig a little deeper into how to use them and how they can help increase productivity.

Goals

Setting goals is foundational to any endeavor. They are the compass that guides your actions, the motivation that fuels your passion, and the benchmark against which you measure progress. Without a clear direction defined by goals, it's too easy to become caught up in busy work, leaving you stranded far from your aspirations.

So, how does one effectively set goals? It's a balance between introspection and envisioning the future you desire.

- **Personal vs. Professional Goals**: While many speak of career aspirations, it's essential to recognize that our personal lives also benefit from goal setting. It isn't always about the next album release, tour, or collaboration. Perhaps it's about buying your first home, exploring different cultures, or achieving that marathon run. Broaden your horizon beyond the professional realm; life is multi-faceted, and your goals should mirror that diversity.

- **SMART Goals:** A practical goal is Specific, Measurable, Achievable, Relevant, and Time-bound. Instead of saying, "I want to be more successful," a SMART goal would be, "I want to release three songs by the end of this summer and perform at five local venues."
- **Alignment with Values:** Your goals should resonate with your core values. If you value family, a goal could be to spend more quality time with them despite a busy schedule. If health is a top priority, setting a fitness goal makes perfect sense.
- **Visualize Success:** Take a moment to picture what achieving that goal would look like. Visualization can be a powerful motivator, driving you forward even on challenging days.
- **Review and Adapt:** As life changes, it's natural for goals to evolve. Regularly revisiting and adjusting your goals ensures they remain relevant and aligned with your current desires and circumstances.

Remember, goals aren't just about the destination but the journey. Each step towards a goal is a testament to your dedication, resilience, and passion.

VALUES

When I started mapping out my life's direction, I realized it wasn't just about setting random goals. It was about anchoring those goals to something deeper, something that defined who I am at my core. And that's how I started understanding the power of values.

What drives you? What are those non-negotiables in your life?

For me, it's the simple things: family moments that make me smile, ensuring my mind and body are in the best shape to take on challenges, and leaving a mark in the music world that feels true to me. It's about my pride in my work's quality and the peace of mind from financial stability. Now, I challenge you to think about it: Grab a notebook and jot down those core beliefs.

Here's the magic: setting goals becomes almost intuitive once you've penned down these values. It's like connecting the dots. Some goals might be right around the corner, while others might be a distant lighthouse. But the journey to each becomes clearer and feels right. And just so you know, we'll get into the nitty-gritty of turning those values into tangible goals in Chapter 4.

TIME BLOCKING

Practicing time blocking was a transformative experience for me. It's all about dedicating specific blocks of time to specific key tasks. This method is a powerful antidote to the lure of multitasking, enabling deep focus on the present task. Consider my meal approach: breakfast, lunch, and dinner are firmly scheduled into my day. These aren't just mealtimes but a testament to my commitment to a consistent and healthy diet, reflecting my broader health priority.

A practical way to implement time blocking is by creating a time map of your ideal week. This isn't about fixing every moment into a rigid schedule but outlining a plan that reflects what your ideal week should look like if all goes to plan. It's a strategy for introspection, helping you to recognize what you might be neglecting, be it those missed lunch breaks, a delayed start to an exercise routine, or even that overdue phone call to a loved one. Strategically incorporating these into your week is a step towards better time management.

The following table (*table 1*) gives you a better idea of what an "Ideal Week Layout" could look like. Remember, this isn't about locking yourself into a rigid timetable. It's about crafting a week where your daily activities resonate with your overarching goals and values, turning each time segment into a meaningful stride toward your goals. I periodically review my Ideal Week Layout, adjusting as necessary to keep my days in sync with the bigger picture. You'll notice there are open slots in this layout. These are for the evolving priorities, unexpected calls, errands, or new projects that pop up. The key here is to ensure that the essentials — those activities that align with your top priorities — are set in place first.

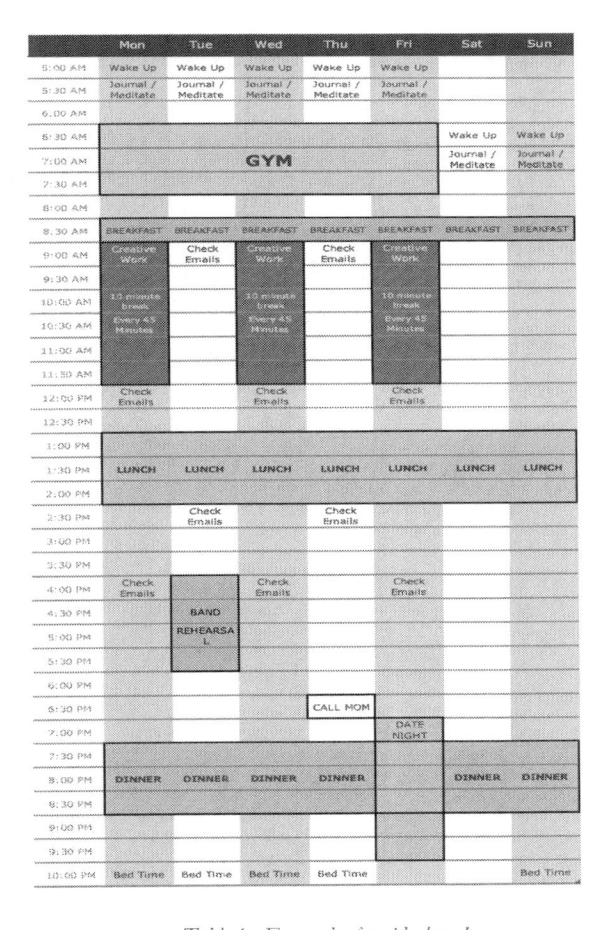

	Mon	Tue	Wed	Thu	Fri	Sat	Sun
5:00 AM	Wake Up	Wake Up	Wake Up	Wake Up	Wake Up		
5:30 AM	Journal / Meditate	Journal / Meditate	Journal / Meditate	Journal / Meditate	Journal / Meditate		
6:00 AM							
6:30 AM						Wake Up	Wake Up
7:00 AM			GYM			Journal / Meditate	Journal / Meditate
7:30 AM							
8:00 AM							
8:30 AM	BREAKFAST	BREAKFAST	BREAKFAST	BREAKFAST	BREAKFAST	BREAKFAST	BREAKFAST
9:00 AM	Creative Work	Check Emails	Creative Work	Check Emails	Creative Work		
9:30 AM							
10:00 AM	10 minute break		10 minute break		10 minute break		
10:30 AM	Every 45 Minutes		Every 45 Minutes		Every 45 Minutes		
11:00 AM							
11:30 AM							
12:00 PM	Check Emails		Check Emails		Check Emails		
12:30 PM							
1:00 PM							
1:30 PM	LUNCH	LUNCH	LUNCH	LUNCH	LUNCH	LUNCH	LUNCH
2:00 PM							
2:30 PM		Check Emails		Check Emails			
3:00 PM							
3:30 PM							
4:00 PM	Check Emails		Check Emails		Check Emails		
4:30 PM		BAND REHEARSAL					
5:00 PM							
5:30 PM							
6:00 PM							
6:30 PM				CALL MOM			
7:00 PM					DATE NIGHT		
7:30 PM							
8:00 PM	DINNER	DINNER	DINNER	DINNER		DINNER	DINNER
8:30 PM							
9:00 PM							
9:30 PM							
10:00 PM	Bed Time	Bed Time	Bed Time	Bed Time			Bed Time

Table 1 - Example of an ideal week.

SET CLEAR BOUNDARIES:

Despite our best efforts to stick to our plans, life often presents unexpected twists and turns. With success comes an increased demand for your time, so establishing boundaries is crucial.

To truly create, you must place yourself in a receptive state, unhindered by distractions. While silencing phone notifications is a step in the right direction, other methods exist to help maintain these boundaries. One technique I swear by is designating specific time blocks solely for creativity. At first, it may seem counterintuitive — can creativity indeed be scheduled? In a way, yes. While you can't always control when inspiration strikes, you can set aside dedicated time, free from external disturbances, to clear your mind and immerse yourself in the creative process. By tuning into the energies around you, you allow creativity to flow naturally. Incorporate these creative sessions as a cornerstone of your ideal week, treating them with the same commitment as any other appointment. Over time, your mind will eagerly anticipate these moments.

> *Mastering the art of saying 'no' to distractions that divert you from your objectives is challenging yet invaluable.*

Use the tools:

Navigating the daily intricacies as a creative can often feel like a balancing act, where each tool you select plays a pivotal role in aligning your daily tasks with your long-term aspirations. Take Google Calendar, for example. It's more than just a planner; it's a platform where you can sketch the larger picture of your life. Creating multiple calendars allows you to take a layered approach: one calendar for personal reminders, another for tracking your ongoing projects, and a third for your "Ideal Week Layout." This method is about setting intentional goals rather than confining yourself to a rigid schedule. You gain insights into how well your actual week aligns with your ideal one by toggling between these views.

There's something uniquely satisfying about the physical act of writing. Using a notebook for jotting down tasks or thoughts is more than a mere exercise; it's about bringing your dreams to life. Ideas that remain in your head do not exist in the real world; writing them down is the first step in making them real.

I also rely on digital tools like Trello and Evernote to stay organized and focused. These tools are helpful, but they're just that – tools. They're there to amplify your goals and visions but shouldn't dominate your creative process. The key is in striking the right balance and finding a way to blend the ease of digital tools with the tangible, personal touch of traditional methods. Each task, note, and goal should resonate with your creative journey.

Here's a quick summary of how I use some of my favorite tools in my daily routine:

- **Google Calendar:** Start your week with it. Every Sunday evening, dedicate some time to lay out your week ahead. Not just the tasks, but also those precious moments of solitude or even a coffee catch-up. As your week unfolds, it's easy to adjust and adapt. The layered calendars provide perspective, letting you see both the micro and macro of your life, so you never lose sight of the larger composition.
- **Notebook and Pen:** This is your daily companion. At the start of your day, scribble down your thoughts, tasks, or any bursts of inspiration. And before bedtime, take a few moments to reflect and jot down any lingering thoughts or ideas. This ritual not only helps keep track but also provides a moment of stillness amid the chaos, acting as bookends to your day.
- **Trello and Evernote:** Use these during your designated admin times. Maybe it's every Wednesday afternoon or perhaps the last hour of your working day. Create boards for different projects on Trello, setting tasks and deadlines. Evernote acts as your digital scratchpad; a space to capture fleeting thoughts, lyrics, or potential collaboration ideas.

Remember, the effectiveness of these tools isn't in the tools themselves, but in how they harmonize with your individual workflow. Their true strength comes to light when you tailor them to fit your personal pace and style, ensuring that every task and every goal aligns seamlessly with your overall objectives.

SPECIFIC METHODS

In our time management learning, we'll encounter many methods, each with its own approach. There's an entire universe of literature on this topic, but I want to zero in on the techniques that are especially valuable for those in the creative field. These aren't your run-of-the-mill time management tricks; they're about fostering creativity and turning your artistic visions into tangible achievements.

FIND YOUR FLOW: THE POMODORO TECHNIQUE

Enter the world of classical musicians and frequently encounter the Pomodoro Technique. Stemming from the Italian term for 'tomato,' this method involves dedicated 25-minute work stints, termed 'pomodoros,' punctuated by a 5-minute respite. It's a rhythm that keeps the mind sharp. For musicians, it means a deep dive into their craft, punctuated by brief moments to breathe and reset.

Prioritizing Tasks: The Eisenhower Matrix

A gem in task management is the Eisenhower Matrix, which classifies tasks by urgency and importance.

Urgent and Important: These are tasks demanding immediate attention.

Real World Example

> Alex, an independent musician, receives an email in the morning informing her that there's an issue with the audio quality of her track, which is set to release tomorrow. Addressing this becomes her top priority.

Not Urgent but Important: These are critical tasks that don't have pressing deadlines.

Real World Example

> Alex knows she needs to plan the marketing for her album release two months from now. It's crucial, but she doesn't need to finalize it today.

Urgent but Not Important: These tasks might seem pressing but can be delegated to someone else.

Real World Example

> Alex gets numerous notifications from her social media pages. While responding to fans is essential, she delegates this task to her manager for the day so she can focus on more pressing matters.

Neither Urgent nor Important: These tasks or activities don't contribute significantly to your primary goals.

Real World Example

> Alex sees an invitation to a non-music-related webinar that piques her interest. While it might be intriguing, attending it won't advance her immediate career goals. She decides to pass.

By categorizing tasks this way, you ensure your energy is focused where it truly counts.

The 2-Minute Rule

We've all been there—facing a task that seems daunting, only to find it's actually relatively brief. The 2-minute rule addresses this: tackle a task immediately if it can be wrapped up in under two minutes. For creatives, this is invaluable. Maybe it's refining a soundbite or capturing a spontaneous lyric. Address it immediately, ensuring such tasks don't morph into distractions.

> **Real World Example**
>
> While Alex is setting up her studio equipment for a recording session, she remembers that she needs to confirm her availability for a podcast interview next week. Rather than postponing it or assuming she'll remember to do it later, she quickly grabs her phone and sends a short confirmation email to the podcast host.

This task, which took less than two minutes, ensured she didn't keep the host waiting and risked forgetting about it amidst her other responsibilities. By doing so, Alex keeps her commitments in check and frees her mind to focus on the recording at hand without a nagging thought in the back of her mind.

Time Blocking

Earlier, I introduced the concept of time blocking—dedicating specific timeframes to particular tasks. It ensures critical tasks aren't overshadowed by trivialities. For example, reserving 9 a.m. to 11 a.m. exclusively for lyric composition. Now, while the 2-minute rule and time blocking might seem at odds, they can harmoniously co-exist:

- **Integration:** Tackle 2-minute tasks as they arise during your time blocks.
- **Dedicated Time:** Set aside specific time blocks to manage an array of 2-minute tasks.
- **Stay Adaptable:** Time blocking is a tool, not an unbreakable law. It's there to aid, not constrict.
- **Evaluation:** If 2-minute tasks frequently disrupt your flow, they may warrant their own time block.

By implementing time blocking into her schedule, Alex can dedicate her full attention to each activity without feeling pulled in multiple directions. It not only boosts her productivity but also gives her a clear sense of purpose for each day.

Keep it Together: Task Batching

Imagine channeling your energy into cohesive task groups instead of sporadically flitting between them. This is task batching—grouping similar tasks to streamline focus. In the studio, for instance, instead of sporadically checking emails, you could allocate an hour solely for that, followed by an uninterrupted lyric-writing session.

While similar, task batching and time blocking aren't identical twins. Task batching clusters tasks by type, say, all creative endeavors in the morning and administrative duties in the afternoon. Time-blocking, however, allocates specific times to these batched tasks.

Both techniques strive to amplify productivity—one by task type, the other by time allocation.

Real World Example

> For Alex, juggling her responsibilities as a musician, songwriter, and entrepreneur often felt like a never-ending game of catch-up. She'd find herself shifting gears constantly, moving from songwriting to answering emails, then to business calls, and back to her guitar. The constant task-switching drained her energy and creativity. That's when she decided to try task batching.

Mornings *(9:00 am - 12:00 pm)* - Creative Work:

- **Songwriting:** Alex sets aside her mornings solely for songwriting. She finds that her creativity is at its peak during these hours. With her phone on "Do Not Disturb" mode, she dives deep into the world of melodies and lyrics.
- **Guitar Practice:** After her songwriting session, Alex practices her guitar, working on new chords or refining existing ones.

Early Afternoon *(1:00 pm - 3:00 pm)* - Business Tasks:

- **Emails:** Alex dedicates this time to answer all her business-related emails. This includes coordinating with event organizers, responding to fan mails, and managing collaboration requests.
- **Booking Shows and Tours:** She looks into available dates, manages her calendar, and contacts venues or organizers, ensuring her shows are lined up and well-coordinated.

Late Afternoon *(3:30 pm - 5:00 pm)* - Communication and Planning:

- **Social media:** Instead of being sporadically active on social media throughout the day, Alex batches

her time to engage with her fans, post updates, and share snippets of her work.
- **Planning and Organization:** Alex reviews her upcoming week, jotting down important dates, planning her studio sessions, and noting down any new song ideas or inspirations.

Time	MONDAY TASK BATCH Task
6:00 AM	Rise and Receive
7:00 AM	
8:00 AM	Creative Work
9:00 AM	
10:00 AM	
11:00 AM	
12:00 PM	LUNCH
1:00 PM	Business Tasks
2:00 PM	
3:00 PM	Communication & Planning
4:00 PM	
5:00 PM	
6:00 PM	
7:00 PM	Dinner
8:00 PM	Downtime / Unwind
9:00 PM	
10:00 PM	
11:00 PM	

Table 2 - Alex's Task Batching for Mondays

As seen on *(table 2)*, by batching similar tasks together, Alex found that she could dive deeper into her work without the mental strain of constantly switching contexts. Her days became more productive, her mind clearer, and her creative output significantly improved.

Remember the importance of rest and introspection. Continually measure your methods and adjust when necessary. A refreshed mind isn't just productive—it's a beacon of creativity. While optimizing time is pivotal, knowing when to pause is equally paramount.

Chapter 2 Summary

In our intricate journey, balancing time management has often been a challenge I've grappled with, a sentiment I'm sure many of you share. In my quest for rhythm, I learned that accurate alignment doesn't just mean managing hours but ensuring they reflect my core values and dreams.

This chapter explored tools like the Pomodoro Technique, a tried-and-true method that emphasizes focused work sessions. We also tackled the Eisenhower Matrix, helping us discern tasks' urgency and importance. Recognizing the significance of addressing small tasks promptly, we discussed the 2-minute Rule. We looked into Time Blocking and Task Batching to prevent our days from feeling scattered, aiming to create a streamlined workflow.

We also explored some of my favorite tools:

- Google Calendar for setting the tempo of our week.

- The tangible connection of pen and paper for our daily reflections.
- Digital aides like Trello and Evernote to anchor our plans and jot down our ideas.

And as we review these strategies, it's essential to remember the value of rest. A refreshed mind isn't merely efficient—it's a vessel for innovation and creativity.

Key Takeaways:

- **Aligning Time and Values:** Reflect on your core values to set the right direction and goals.
- **Pomodoro Technique:** Focus for 25 minutes, then take a breather.
- **Eisenhower Matrix:** Prioritize tasks effectively.
- **The 2-Minute Rule:** Address small tasks immediately to keep momentum.
- **Time Blocking:** Dedicate set hours to specific tasks for a structured day.
- **Task Batching:** Group similar tasks for efficiency.
- **Tools in the Kit:** Google Calendar, notebook, pen, Trello, and Evernote.
- **Value of Rest:** Embrace breaks and downtime to rejuvenate your mind.

In conclusion, the insights and tools discussed in this chapter are designed to empower you to steer your days purposefully. They're meant to align your daily actions with larger aspirations, enabling you to move forward with intention and clarity.

3

NURTURING CREATIVITY WHILE OWNING YOUR TIME

At first glance, time management and creativity might seem at odds. The free spirit of creativity often feels constrained by the regimented beats of time management. But if there's one group that truly understands the relationship between time and artistry, it's musicians.

Consider music: a combination of sound and rhythm. Each beat, note, and harmony plays within the bounds set by time. The ticking metronome isn't a tool of restriction; instead, it's the heartbeat of every tune. From classical orchestrations to modern anthems, time serves not as a constraint but as a stage for harmonies, lyrics, and melodies to shine.

Beyond music, there's the universe's natural symphony. Sacred geometry, the universe's patterned language, is evident everywhere—from the Fibonacci sequence in blooming flowers to the vast spirals of galaxies. The golden ratio, revered as beauty's mathematical essence, intertwines deeply with time. Our world's wonders, be it nature's bloom or the celestial dance, operate in meticulous timing. This grand synchronicity showcases how structure doesn't restrict; it amplifies.

Translating this to our creative pursuits reveals that time is not our cage but our canvas. It offers the vast space upon which we craft our masterpieces. Proper time management, then, isn't about stifling our inner muse but about setting a stage for her. It's about crafting a rhythm, a guiding pulse, for our passions. Just as a composer leverages time signatures and scales to craft sonatas, we, too, can channel our creativity more effectively by valuing time.

SO, HOW DOES TIME MANAGEMENT SERVE AS A STIMULUS FOR CREATIVITY?

Think of it as the frame that gives a painting its form, the structure enabling an artist's vision to take flight. When we're consistent in our creative pursuits, it's like setting a rhythmic rendezvous with our muse; these meetings deepen with time and repetition. Passion might be the driving force, but it's essential to remember our own well-being. Structured breaks and dedicated work periods ensure we're always at our best, ready to tackle our craft with renewed energy. Moments set aside for reflection let us visualize our journey, acknowledge our successes and understand our challenges. When merged, time management and creativity dance a harmonious duet, leading to results that are both effective and filled with inspiration.

Setting Boundaries for Creative Freedom

I've always been meticulous about the environment in which I immerse myself during my creative pursuits. Everything matters—the ambiance, the lighting, even the very aroma that fills the space. Whether it's a conscious decision or an intuitive one, what we're truly doing is aligning our surroundings for optimal reception. We're creating a boundary, shielding ourselves from the chaos outside, ensuring the only noises we hear are the melodies of our own thoughts and creativity. Just as prominent recording studios pour resources into crafting the perfect, distraction-free zones, we, too, must recognize the value in doing so. Designating a physical and mental space for creativity is crucial, but carving out time for it is just as essential.

Physical and Temporal Boundaries

The physical environment is crucial in harnessing one's potential in any art form. Think of an artist's studio filled with canvases, paints, and brushes or a writer's den with shelves of books and a dedicated writing desk. These spaces are sanctuaries, free from the noise of the outside world. Just the act of entering such spaces signals our brain that it's time to create. The environment we curate is not just about aesthetics; it's about crafting a personalized zone that aligns with our creative spirit.

Mental Boundaries:

In today's digital age, our minds are continually bombarded with information, making it challenging to find a quiet space for thoughts to flow. Setting mental boundaries means decluttering the mind. It's about creating a mental sanctuary, free from the chaos of daily life, where ideas can germinate and grow. Techniques like meditation, mindfulness, and even simple breathing exercises can be instrumental in achieving this.

Emotional Boundaries

As artists, feedback is our compass. It directs, refines, and sometimes even reshapes our work. However, it's essential to differentiate between constructive insights and mere noise. Embracing critiques that elevate our work while guarding against negativity is the balance we must strive for, ensuring our core creative essence remains untarnished.

Boundary Between Work and Rest

Visualize an audio waveform. The peaks and valleys represent the ebb and flow of sound, much like our creative energies. No song is a continuous peak; that would be overwhelming and monotonous. Instead, the interplay between these highs and lows, the crescendos and the quiet moments, creates a harmonic balance.

Similarly, our creative process isn't about maintaining a constant peak of productivity. It's about embracing the natural rhythm of intense creativity (the peaks) and moments of rest and rejuvenation (the valleys). Just as an audio waveform provides structure to a track, understanding when to work and rest provides structure to our creativity.

Think of it this way: Continuous sound at one frequency becomes noise. Similarly, unceasing work without breaks can lead to a static-like stagnation in creativity. By distinguishing between intense creativity and relaxation periods, we emulate the audio waveform's balance. This helps prevent burnout and ensures that, much like the following note in a song, we approach our craft with fresh eyes and a renewed spirit.

Boundaries aren't shackles; they're the unsung guides. They channel, focus, and elevate our creative energies, acting as the compass in our artistic journey. As we tread this path, let's embrace these boundaries, acknowledging their role in steering us toward unparalleled brilliance.

COMBINING TIME MANAGEMENT AND CREATIVE WORK.

Balancing time management and creativity has always been like threading a needle for me. It's been a mix of lessons learned, happy accidents, and some real "aha!" moments. Over the years, I've found ways that seamlessly blend the discipline of time with the freedom of creativity. Up next are some of my go-to exercises that have made all the difference. I encourage you to give them a shot, maybe even put your own spin on them, and see how they can kick your creative energy up a notch.

The Creative Power Hour

- Choose a time during the day when you feel the most energetic and alert. Mark it on your calendar as your "Creative Power Hour."
- During this hour, focus solely on a creative task—brainstorming, sketching, writing, or composing.
- Eliminate all distractions. Put your phone on airplane mode, close unrelated tabs on your computer, and inform anyone around you that you shouldn't be disturbed.
- At the end of the hour, jot down what you accomplished.

The 15-Minute Brain Dump

- Set aside 15 minutes every morning or evening.
- Grab a notebook and write down everything on your mind—ideas, worries, tasks.
- This process clears mental clutter, making space for creative thoughts to flourish.

Scheduled Breaks for Inspiration

- During your workday, set a timer to take a 10-minute break every hour.

- During these breaks, do something unrelated to your work. Take a walk, listen to music, or do some light stretching.
- These moments of pause can often lead to unexpected sparks of inspiration.

TIME-BOXED EXPLORATION

- Dedicate a block of time, say 30 minutes to an hour, once a week to explore something new. This could be a new art form, a book outside your usual genre, or even a documentary on a topic you know nothing about.
- Diversifying your experiences can lead to fresh perspectives and ideas.

REFLECTIVE JOURNALING

- Spend 10 minutes at the end of your day journaling about what went well, what challenges you faced, and any new ideas or insights you had.
- This records your growth and helps you recognize patterns, habits, or triggers that influence your creative process.

The Two-Day Idea Rule

- Jot a new idea down in a dedicated notebook or digital note-taking app whenever it strikes.
- Revisit the idea two days later. This gap allows your subconscious mind to work on it, often leading to richer development or new angles.

The Creative Swap

- Swap between multiple creative projects at set intervals if you're involved in numerous creative projects. For instance, if you're writing and dabbling in graphic design, switch between these tasks every other day.
- This keeps your creative juices flowing and ensures you don't burn out on a single project.

Incorporating these exercises into your daily or weekly routine can be a game-changer. Not only will they enhance your creativity, but they'll also help you manage your time more efficiently. It's all about giving structure to spontaneity, ensuring that your creative flame burns bright without burning out.

Chapter Summary:

This chapter explored the harmonious interplay between time management and creativity. Far from contradictory, these elements intertwine like rhythm and melody in a beautiful symphony. We examined how setting boundaries can ignite our creative flames, highlighting the importance of finding the perfect balance where discipline meets passion and creativity soars.

Key Takeaways:

- **Balance is Key:** Time management and creativity aren't enemies; they're allies. Like the rhythm section in a band, they work in synch.
- **Boundaries Boost Creativity:** Designating a creative space, both in terms of environment and time, sets the stage for your muse to shine.
- **Rest and Workflow:** Think of your work and rest periods like the peaks and troughs of an audio waveform, both essential for creating the perfect sound.
- **Practical Techniques Matter:** Tried and tested exercises can help bridge the structured world of time with the expansive realm of creativity.

- **Reflection is Growth:** Taking time to assess and introspect is invaluable. It's through understanding our past efforts that we carve out a clearer path forward.

4

SETTING, PRIORITIZING AND CRUSHING YOUR GOALS

Before we get started with prioritization, let's take a moment to shine a light on two terms that often walk the halls of our discussions: 'goals' and 'priorities.' They might casually be tossed into the same basket but serve distinct roles in guiding our efforts. Understanding their differences empowers us to make informed decisions, directing our time and energy more efficiently. So, let's shed light on these concepts and see how they add to our journey.

GOALS:

- A goal is a specific outcome or result you want to achieve within a set timeframe. It's the endpoint or destination of a particular journey or endeavor.
- Goals are often measurable and have clear success criteria. For example, "Release an album by the end of the year" or "Tour three new cities in the next six months."
- Goals have a start and an end. Once achieved, a goal is either marked as completed or evolves into a new goal based on subsequent aspirations.

PRIORITIES:

- A priority is about establishing importance or precedence among various tasks, projects, or goals. It helps you decide where to focus your time, energy, and resources at any given moment.
- Priorities can shift based on circumstances, immediate needs, or changing environments. While working towards releasing an album, an artist might prioritize songwriting in one phase and recording in another.
- Priorities are dynamic and can change more frequently than goals. As situations evolve, what's deemed most important can shift.

In simple terms:

> *A **goal** is what you want to achieve.*
> *A **priority** is about determining the order or importance of reaching various goals or completing specific tasks.*

Remember our musician friend, Alex? She's set a clear, ambitious goal: releasing her second album in the next 18 months. Alex has many other aspirations – from touring new cities to personal endeavors like picking up a new instrument. However, this new album has the potential to propel her career to new heights and has taken center stage.

In pursuit of this dream, her priorities are laser focused. Amidst a sea of tasks and commitments, she dedicates considerable time to songwriting, seeking collaborations with artists who align with her musical vision, investing in studio time, and planning subsequent promotional campaigns. Every decision, every priority, is a calculated move, inching her closer to that album release date. It's a vivid demonstration of how setting clear priorities can guide our actions and help us achieve our most desired goals.

PRIORITIZATION TOOLS AND TECHNIQUES

In any craft, time management included, essential tools and techniques are available for specific tasks. A painter relies on brushes, a musician on their instrument, each tool carefully chosen for its purpose. Similarly, in time management, selecting the right resources is vital. You wouldn't use a guitar pick to carve a marble sculpture. To find what best aligns with your workflow, it's equally important to experiment with various tools, even if they serve similar functions. The goal is to ensure the tool enhances, rather than overshadows, the task at hand. Join me as we explore the techniques and tools I've cherished and used to set my priorities straight.

THE ABCD TECHNIQUE

Prioritizing tasks can sometimes feel overwhelming, but the ABCD technique, also known as *The Eisenhower Method*, breaks it down, making it digestible and actionable. Here's how it works:

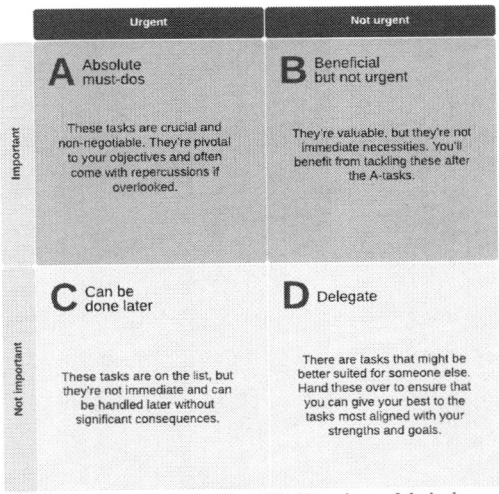

	Urgent	Not urgent
Important	**A** Absolute must-dos — These tasks are crucial and non-negotiable. They're pivotal to your objectives and often come with repercussions if overlooked.	**B** Beneficial but not urgent — They're valuable, but they're not immediate necessities. You'll benefit from tackling these after the A-tasks.
Not important	**C** Can be done later — These tasks are on the list, but they're not immediate and can be handled later without significant consequences.	**D** Delegate — There are tasks that might be better suited for someone else. Hand these over to ensure that you can give your best to the tasks most aligned with your strengths and goals.

Figure 1 ABCD... The Eisenhower Method

The Eisenhower method (*fig. 1*) offers a guide to navigate your tasks with precision. By categorizing tasks this way, you clearly identify where to direct your efforts, enhancing your productivity. Tackling essential tasks first ensures nothing crucial gets overlooked. This method also aids in effective delegation and battles procrastination, blending structure with adaptability. And as you regularly employ this technique, your decision-making sharpens, always steering your focus to the most pressing matters. In essence, the ABCD Technique not only boosts efficiency but also provides relief from the chaos of daily tasks.

Digital Aids for Prioritization

In an age with an app for almost everything, it shouldn't be a surprise that terrific digital tools are explicitly designed to assist us in prioritization. Beyond just setting reminders or jotting down to-dos, these tools harness the power of technology to make the task of prioritizing not just more accessible but also more intuitive and efficient.

While many of us might be familiar with standard task management apps, there's a whole world of advanced features that can push your prioritization game to new heights:

Hierarchical Tasks

Some apps allow for tasks to be broken down into subtasks, ensuring you see the larger picture while not losing sight of the finer details.

Here are some of my favorite apps that can help you do just that:

- **Todoist**: This app allows you to create projects, and within those projects, you can have tasks and sub-tasks. It also supports priority levels, giving a clear view of what needs immediate attention.
- **Trello**: Using a board, list, and card system, Trello lets users break down tasks hierarchically. Cards can have checklists that further split tasks into smaller actionable items.
- **Microsoft To Do:** Evolved from the Wunderlist app, Microsoft To Do allows for list creation, and within those lists, you can add tasks and further break them down into steps.
- **Notion:** A versatile workspace tool, Notion supports a wide array of task management features, including the creation of tasks and sub-tasks using nested toggle lists or databases.
- **Things 3:** Exclusively for Apple devices, Things 3 offers a clean interface where tasks can be broken down into smaller parts and can be organized by areas, projects, and individual to-dos.
- **ClickUp:** Touted as a "one app to replace them all", ClickUp offers detailed task breakdowns. Tasks can have sub-tasks, and those sub-tasks can even have their own sub-tasks.

Visual Representations

Think kanban boards, Gantt charts, and mind maps. These visual tools allow you to easily see your thoughts, allowing you to make adjustments as necessary.

- **Trello:** Its card-based system is intuitive and allows for a clear visual representation of task progression across columns.
- **Airtable:** This unique tool combines spreadsheet simplicity with database complexity, offering grid, calendar, kanban, and gallery views of data.
- **MindMeister:** A leading mind mapping tool, it allows users to visually plot out ideas and tasks in a branching, hierarchical manner.
- **Asana:** While it offers list-based views, it also provides a board view and timeline view, making it a diverse tool for visual task management.
- **Notion:** Blending traditional note taking and task management, Notion provides a range of visual tools, including boards

Integrations

The ability to mesh with other apps and tools means your prioritization app isn't an isolated island but part of a synchronized ecosystem.

Let's consider Alex's process of coordinating her team. Managing everyone, from the songwriters and producers to the marketing mavens, isn't just about her musical prowess. It's about weaving together the right tools seamlessly.

- **Google Workspace:** Alex starts drafting album concepts and lyrics in Google Docs. Given her team's diverse locations, the real-time collaboration feature lets everyone chime in, no matter where they are.
- **Slack:** Alex shares the document link in their dedicated album Slack channel once they've settled on a direction. Thanks to Slack's Google Drive integration, the team can view and discuss the document from the chat. Additionally, they use Slack channels to brainstorm marketing strategies, plan the album tour, and discuss merchandise ideas.
- **Trello:** To manage the many tasks leading up to the album launch, Alex creates a Trello board. Every song, every promotional activity, and every tour date is represented by a card. Using the Google Calendar Power-Up, Alex ensures that any deadlines or key dates are mirrored in her personal calendar.
- **Zapier:** Recognizing the importance of fan engagement, Alex sets up a Zap. Whenever a new tour date is added to Trello, Zapier automatically posts an update to her fan email list through MailChimp, ensuring her fans are always in the loop.
- **Asana:** The marketing team swears by Asana for detailed task tracking. With Google Workspace

integration, they can easily link to the original strategy docs. They track press releases, interviews, and social media campaigns, ensuring no opportunity is missed.

This interconnected setup keeps Alex and her team on the same page and streamlines their efforts. Each tool plays its part, and integrations ensure they work harmoniously, much like the instruments in one of Alex's songs.

THE EISENHOWER MATRIX IN ACTION: ALEX'S 2ND ALBUM

Though we brushed upon the Eisenhower method in an earlier chapter, there's nothing quite like seeing it in action. *Figure 3* on the next page gives us a look at how Alex leverages the ABCD technique to prioritize tasks for her album release. It's a method I swear by, having used it time and again for both my personal and professional goals. Dive in and see if it resonates with you as it did for me.

Using the Eisenhower method, Alex can not only categorize tasks but execute them efficiently. This framework keeps her focused on what truly matters while effectively managing her time and resources.

Urgent

A. Absolute must-dos

Finalize the Mixes — With a tight release schedule, Alex can't afford delays. The final mix of her tracks needs immediate attention.

Album Artwork Approvals — The graphics team needs her go-ahead to finalize the cover art and promotional material.

Not urgent

B. Beneficial but not urgent

Songwriting Sessions — While the album is in its final stages, Alex knows she needs to keep the creative juices flowing for future projects.

Vocal Training — Regular sessions with her coach ensure she's in top form, both for the album and upcoming tours.

Urgent — Not important

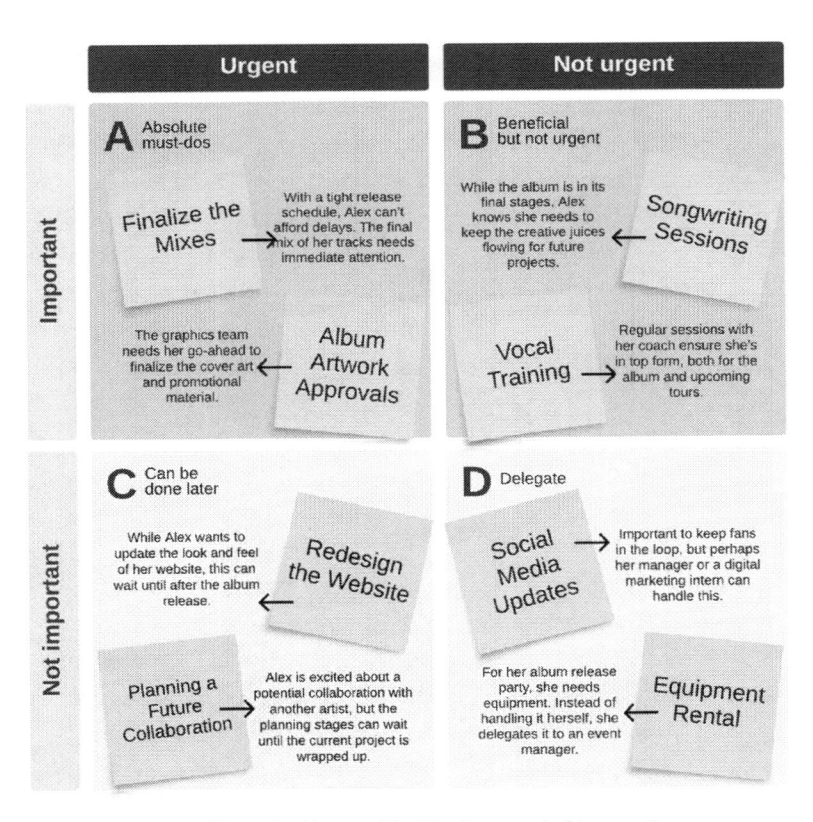

C. Can be done later

Redesign the Website — While Alex wants to update the look and feel of her website, this can wait until after the album release.

Planning a Future Collaboration — Alex is excited about a potential collaboration with another artist, but the planning stages can wait until the current project is wrapped up.

Not urgent — Not important

D. Delegate

Social Media Updates — Important to keep fans in the loop, but perhaps her manager or a digital marketing intern can handle this.

Equipment Rental — For her album release party, she needs equipment. Instead of handling it herself, she delegates it to an event manager.

Figure 3 Alex puts The Eisenhower method into practice

Quick Prioritization Hacks:

The 2-Minute Rule:

Revisiting the 2-Minute Rule from our earlier discussion on time management is crucial, especially as we focus on prioritization. This small yet impactful technique significantly clears up task clutter and sharpens focus on what truly matters.

Here's the Rule in its simplest form: if a task can be done in 2 minutes or less, do it immediately. This practice effectively removes smaller tasks from your agenda, allowing you more mental space and time to concentrate on larger, more complex tasks. It's a straightforward habit change, but the sense of achievement it brings can significantly boost your motivation and productivity.

The Ivy Lee Method:

At the end of each day, jot down six essential tasks for the following day. Then prioritize them in order of importance. Start the next day working on the top task, moving to the next only when it's finished. This method ensures you address the most critical tasks first, leading to a more structured and productive day.

Mind Mapping in Minutes:

A mind map (see *fig 4*) is a visual treat for the brainstormer. Think of it as doodling with purpose. At its core, it's about branching out your ideas from a central topic, connecting related thoughts, and visualizing the hierarchy or flow between them. For instance, if Alex were to mind map her album launch, she'd start with "Album Launch" in the center. Branching out might be categories like "Promotion," "Song Finalization," and "Collaborations." Under "Promotion," she could have "Social Media," "Radio Play," and "Interviews." It's a quick way to see the big picture, understand how tasks interrelate, and, most importantly, figure out where to pour your energies first.

Figure 4 Example of Alex's Mind Map

Navigating through multiple tools and techniques, each with unique names and promises, can feel like being handed a new instrument for every note in a song. It might seem overwhelming at first glance. However, just as a musician doesn't play every instrument simultaneously, you don't need to use all these tools simultaneously. See them as items in your creative toolkit, ready and waiting. You don't pull out every tool for every task, but by knowing they're there, you're prepared. So, when the time is right, you'll intuitively reach for what you need, ensuring your path remains clear, your focus sharp, and your creativity unrestrained.

CHAPTER SUMMARY

- **Goals vs. Priorities:** While goals set our destination, priorities determine our journey's route. They are the markers and steps we take to reach our desired end. Using Alex's example, we delved into how her aim of releasing her second album dictated her priorities, emphasizing the importance of aligning tasks with bigger aspirations.
- **Prioritization Tools and Techniques:** From the foundational ABCD technique to the power of modern digital aids, we dove deep into the tools that can structure our priorities. The digital realm offers vast possibilities, from apps that visualize our tasks to integrations that streamline our processes.

- **The Eisenhower Method - Alex's Take:** Revisiting the Eisenhower method, we walked alongside Alex to see how she employed this strategy in her journey towards her album release.
- **Quick Prioritization Hacks:** We brushed up on the 2-Minute Rule and introduced the Ivy Lee Method. Additionally, we explored the clarity mind mapping can provide in minutes.

Key Takeaways:

- Prioritization is not just about what we do but the order in which we tackle them.
- The right tools, while valuable, are most effective when used appropriately.
- Even amid an ocean of tasks, focusing on priorities ensures we stay directed towards our overarching goals.
- The beauty of these tools and techniques lies in their adaptability. They are the instruments in our creative symphony, ready to be played when the moment is right.

5

From Planning to Execution

We've all heard it a million times: "If you fail to plan, you plan to fail." Yeah, it's overused, but there's a reason it's been around for so long. There's some solid truth in there. Life throws curveballs, and while it's fun to hit a few out of the park on a whim, most times, it's our preparation that sets us up for the win.

I'm not saying you must have every second of your day mapped out. That's just unrealistic. But let's bring this down to the daily grind, too. When I look at my day, I aim to plan about 80% of it, leaving a solid chunk—20%—for those unexpected moments, last-minute meetings, or even just some spontaneous downtime. It's like having a safety net for your day. It's the same principle for the bigger picture: I've got a grip on 80% of my week, and then the weekends? They're my wildcard. It's a balance, a mix of the structured and the spontaneous.

But here's the catch – what good is a plan if it's just gathering dust? A plan without action is like a car without an engine. It might look good, but it's not going anywhere. So, while planning is a big piece of the puzzle, execution is the game-changer. That's where the magic happens.

In this chapter, we're diving deep. We'll discuss the nuts and bolts of laying out a solid plan. But more importantly, we'll tackle how to stick to it and make it come alive. You're in the right place if you're looking for no-nonsense advice on getting stuff done and making the most of your time. Let's roll up our sleeves and get to it.

UNDERSTANDING THE CREATIVE JOURNEY

Reading Rick Rubin's "The Creative Way" was enlightening. Rubin unravels the intricate tapestry of creativity, discussing its beauty, the introspection it demands, and its inherent vulnerabilities. But there's an underline to his narrative: time doesn't pause for our creative whims. It's always moving, and commitments and schedules are waiting on the other side.

So, here's the thing. As creators, we're caught in this dance—crafting our art while racing against the clock. It's a challenge but also an art in itself. We must be intentional with our time, setting tangible goals while embracing the unexpected detours that often define the creative journey.

Our world is one of fluidity and change. Static schedules? They just won't cut it. Instead, our plans should be adaptable, ready to evolve with the rhythm of our creativity. And when we stumble—and trust me, we will—our adaptability and resilience are what will pick us back up.

This discussion sets the stage for what's to come in this book. We're not merely talking about managing time; we're looking at how to flourish creatively within its framework. As we progress, let's leverage Rubin's insights, weaving them into our approach to time management, blending discipline with creativity to compose a harmonious life where time is respected and creatively utilized.

DEFINE CLEAR GOALS

Okay, let's chat about something pivotal: direction. Imagine setting out on a cross-country road trip without a map. You've got the snacks, the tunes, the company — but no clue where you're heading. Sounds adventurous? Maybe. Productive? Doubtful.

First up, you've got to establish your "why". This isn't just a fun tagline for a motivational poster; it's the backbone of your journey. It's that silent pep-talk you give yourself during challenging times. When your "*why*" and your vision do a little tango dance, they become unstoppable. You're not merely going with the flow but directing the current.

We've talked big picture, but let's zoom in a tad. Grand aspirations are the dream, but you need a strategy broken down into short-term and long-term goals to get there. Consider them your steppingstones, ensuring that you're headed in the right direction with every step. It's not just about the destination but celebrating those little victories.

Now, remember Alex from earlier? Let's dive back into her world for a quick minute. She's on the path to releasing her second album. Big goal? Absolutely. But here's how Alex sets it SMART: *"By next month, I'll have written and polished three new tracks, collaborated with at least two featured artists, and finalized the cover art concept for my album."*

Boom! Specific, Measurable, Achievable, Relevant, and Time-bound. Alex is piecing her dream together, step by strategic step. The image on *figure 5* breaks down this statement to show exactly why it's a SMART goal:

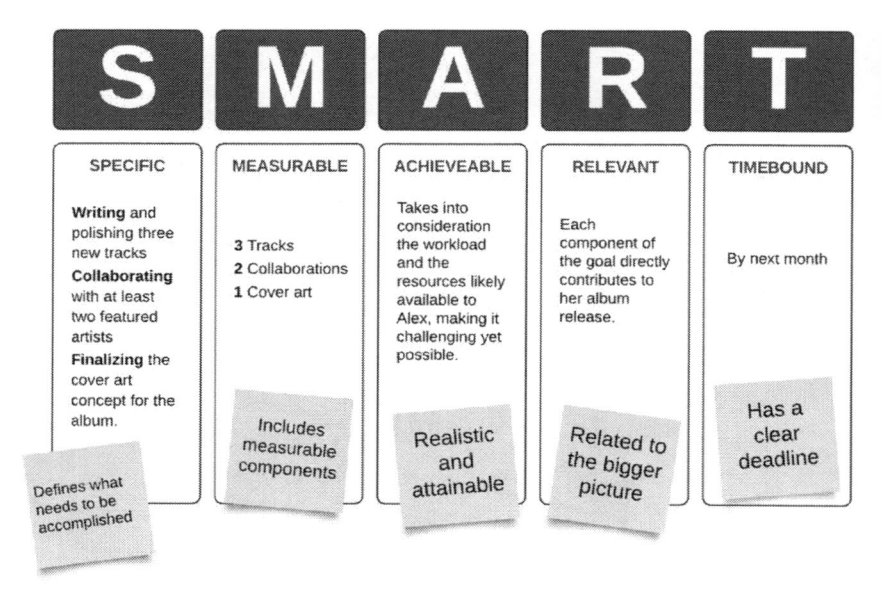

SPECIFIC	MEASURABLE	ACHIEVEABLE	RELEVANT	TIMEBOUND
Writing and polishing three new tracks **Collaborating** with at least two featured artists **Finalizing** the cover art concept for the album.	3 Tracks 2 Collaborations 1 Cover art	Takes into consideration the workload and the resources likely available to Alex, making it challenging yet possible.	Each component of the goal directly contributes to her album release.	By next month
Defines what needs to be accomplished	Includes measurable components	Realistic and attainable	Related to the bigger picture	Has a clear deadline

Figure 5 Be SMART, like Alex

While diving into goals, let's touch on a distinction close to my heart: **macro versus micro goals**. Think of macro goals as your grand visions, the sweeping panoramas of what you want to achieve. For Alex, it was releasing her second album. These big targets might seem distant but guide your every step. Then there are the micro goals, those daily or weekly tasks that are the steppingstones leading to the grander vision. They're the studio sessions, the songwriting afternoons, and the album cover design discussions. It's essential to strike a balance. While macro goals set the direction, micro goals ensure you make tangible progress daily. Both are critical. One sets the dream, the other paves the path. Keep 'em both in sight, and remember, every big dream starts with a single step, and then another, and another... you get the drift.

You might have come across SMART goals in some productivity workshop or another. But trust me, it isn't just corporate jargon. It's like having a GPS for your dreams. Pinpoint accuracy, tailored just for you.

Here's A little secret – it doesn't have to be complicated. I, for one, stick to the classics. This giant dry-erase board in my home office is where I jot down my goals. Plain and simple. But even in its simplicity, every goal I write down checks off those SMART elements. It's all about clarity and drive, not bells and whistles.

CREATE A REALISTIC SCHEDULE

Crafting a schedule is not about cramming every waking hour with tasks, especially when you're a creator. It's about striking a balance, ensuring that your creative juices aren't drained while still hitting those crucial milestones.

Here's the thing about creatives: we don't always adhere to the conventional 9-5 work routine. Alex, for instance, discovered her creativity peaked during late-night sessions. These were her moments of magic. Just as she found her rhythm, you must understand when you're at your creative best.

However, a strict schedule might not always resonate with the unpredictable nature of creativity. Flexibility is the name of the game. This doesn't mean you should drift aimlessly. Instead, create a framework that guides you but leaves enough space for those spontaneous bursts of creativity.

Your mental well-being is paramount. Regular breaks are non-negotiable. Stretch those legs, let your eyes rest, or go for a quick walk. This isn't slacking off; it's essential maintenance for your creative engine.

Now, onto some actionable tips to help you sculpt that realistic schedule:

- **Know Your Prime Time:** Identify your 'golden hour' when creativity flows. Morning sunshine or midnight moonlight, find your prime time.

- **Flexibility is Key:** Stay adaptable. An unexpected collaboration or a eureka moment could emerge. Adjust, but stay aligned with your primary goals.
- **Schedule Breaks:** Take a 15-minute breather. Refresh and re-engage.
- **Prioritize Self-Care:** Remember to recharge those creative batteries through meditation or a leisure day.
- **Use Technology:** Explore apps tailored for creators. They're designed to enhance your workflow.
- **Avoid Multitasking:** Dive deep into one task at a time. Depth over breadth, always.
- **Visualize Your Day:** A visual reminder can anchor you, whether a vision board or a trusty dry-erase board.
- **Set Boundaries:** Designate workspaces and balance passion with personal life.
- **Plan for Downtime:** Give your brain that 'idle' moment; allowing it to intentionally rest can put it at its creative best.
- **Stay Connected:** Regular chats with fellow creators can lead to insights, collaborations, and fresh perspectives.

Given that Alex is a night owl with her peak creativity happening at night, here's an example of Alex's schedule on any given day:

Alex's schedule revolves around her peak creative times. It's a mix of structured tasks and fluid creative moments. What's crucial is that she understands herself and crafts her day to harness her best hours. Your schedule can be different; the key is to make it work for you.

The image on the next page (*fig. 6*) illustrates how Alex can work late, when she is most creative, and still have time for self-care, three meals, breaks, family time, emails, and music. Remember, this is not a one-size-fits-all guide, but a tool that can be personalized to suit your individual circumstances. The key is to be intentional with your time.

FROM PLANNING TO EXECUTION

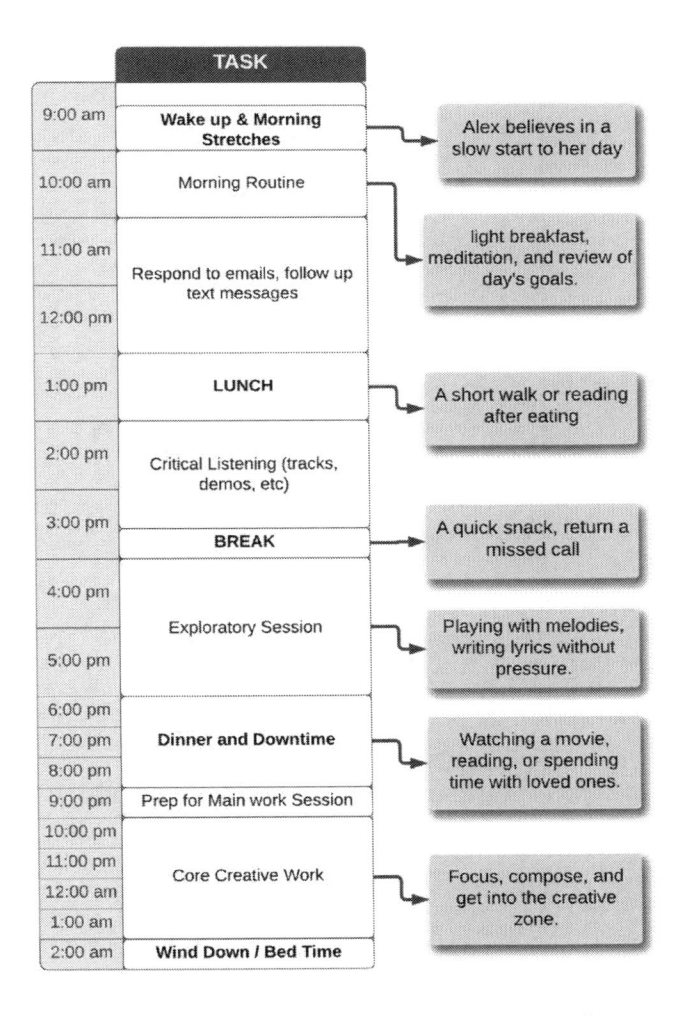

Time	TASK	
9:00 am	Wake up & Morning Stretches	Alex believes in a slow start to her day
10:00 am	Morning Routine	
11:00 am	Respond to emails, follow up text messages	light breakfast, meditation, and review of day's goals.
12:00 pm		
1:00 pm	LUNCH	A short walk or reading after eating
2:00 pm	Critical Listening (tracks, demos, etc)	
3:00 pm	BREAK	A quick snack, return a missed call
4:00 pm	Exploratory Session	Playing with melodies, writing lyrics without pressure.
5:00 pm		
6:00 pm	Dinner and Downtime	Watching a movie, reading, or spending time with loved ones.
7:00 pm		
8:00 pm		
9:00 pm	Prep for Main work Session	
10:00 pm	Core Creative Work	Focus, compose, and get into the creative zone.
11:00 pm		
12:00 am		
1:00 am		
2:00 am	Wind Down / Bed Time	

Figure 6- Alex's creative time block is based on her being a "night owl."

BUILD YOUR SUPPORT SYSTEM

I once sat across from one of my most influential mentors over a casual coffee chat when he leaned in and said, "The music industry is not in your bedroom." Those words resonated with me deeply. While our creativity might originate in isolation, its growth, sustenance, and eventual success lie in our connections with the world outside.

In the hustle of our daily routines, we sometimes forget the immense power of human connection. Understanding that our time isn't just for solo work is essential. It's crucial to carve out specific moments for networking: making that call to a mentor, catching up with colleagues, attending an industry event, or simply brainstorming with a friend. These interactions aren't just breaks but investments in our growth and learning.

FIND YOUR TRIBE

It's tempting, especially in today's digital age, to think we can forge ahead alone. But true success in the creative industry, or any industry for that matter, is often a result of the relationships we build. Whether it's collaborating on a project, brainstorming ideas, or simply having someone who understands the highs and lows of your journey - finding your tribe can make all the difference. Platforms like Clubhouse, LinkedIn, and even Instagram can be a goldmine for networking. Remember, it's not about the number of connections but the quality and depth of those relationships.

The Value of Sharing Experiences

When I think back to the early days of my career, I'm grateful for the guidance I received. Every piece of advice and every shared experience saved me from countless pitfalls. Conversely, as I grew, mentoring became a two-way street. Sharing your knowledge not only uplifts another but also solidifies your own understanding and broadens your perspective. It's a fulfilling cycle: be guided, grow, and then guide others.

Feedback Loops

Let's be honest, no one loves criticism. But here's a twist – constructive criticism is a gift. It's an outsider's perspective, a fresh pair of eyes on what you've been too close to see clearly. Create a circle of trusted individuals who can provide honest feedback about a new project, idea, or even your time management techniques. Listen, reflect, adjust, and grow. It's through these iterative improvements that we inch closer to our vision.

The journey from planning to execution isn't a solitary one. Surrounding yourself with the right people ensures that you make your time count and that the path is a little less rocky and a lot more rewarding.

CONSISTENCY OVER PERFECTION

For creativity, perfection may seem like a good thing, but usually, perfection is the villain of productivity. We're taught in our daily lives to aim for perfection, but what indeed elevates an artist isn't the tiny bits of flawless work; it's the habitual hammering away of their craft. Consistency, therefore, is the actual engine of progress, and discipline and time management are the fuel that drives consistency.

We all have days when the inspiration well seems dry and creating feels more like a chore. It's on these that committing to consistency becomes essential. It's about showing up, putting in the effort, and trusting the process entirely. Perfection may set the bar, but consistency builds the ladder to reach it, one step at a time.

For me, embracing consistency over perfection meant accepting that not every session would produce a hit song. But every session was a step forward, a lesson learned, a skill honed, a vibe felt. This mindset shift is critical: it allows creators to find satisfaction in the act of creation itself rather than being outcome dependent. Create for the process, not for the outcome.

Being consistent also means setting up a schedule that acknowledges our human limitations. It means regular breaks, self-care, and understanding that sometimes, the best thing for our creativity isn't to push forward harder but to step back and recharge. The sustainable effort is worth more than the aggressive jolt.

It's about being kind to ourselves and understanding that while striving for perfection, we must embrace minor victories. The combined effect of consistent work is powerful, and that dedication to the craft often separates the greats from the rest.

By creating a consistent schedule and defining our rhythm, we manage our time and honor our commitment to our art. And that, in turn, lays down the foundation for a legacy of work that outlives us.

TRACK PROGRESS AND CELEBRATE MILESTONES

I accomplished a lot in my 20s, but I didn't feel successful internally. Looking back, I realize I didn't stop to celebrate the small stuff – those little wins in my career. And it wasn't just work; I even let personal stuff like birthdays slide in the name of "getting things done." I was so caught up in the work that I didn't see how far I'd come.

Since then, I've learned that tracking progress is not about obsessing over every detail; it's more about marking the significant milestones that lead you to your goal.

Here's my perspective on this:

- **Set clear markers:** Think of it like checkpoints in a game. They show you're moving in the right direction and give you that little boost every time you hit one.

- **Take time to reflect:** It's like a time-out during a busy day. Ask yourself, "What did I do well?" and "What can I do better?" This can really help steer you right.
- **Celebrate the little things:** Got through a challenging task? Celebrate it. It's these small wins that keep you going.
- **Keep a log:** Write down what you do. It's not just about remembering it; it's about seeing the proof of your hard work overtime.
- **Get input:** A fresh pair of eyes can see things you might miss. So, get feedback; it can be gold.
- **Make milestones matter:** When you hit a big goal, make a thing of it. Have a meal, take a day off, and tell people about it. It matters.
- **Be ready to change it up:** Goals change as you grow, and that's okay. Adjusting your aim isn't failing; it's being smart.

It's about where you're going and how you get there. By paying attention to your progress and giving yourself a pat on the back now and then, you're not just getting stuff done – you're building a story you'll be proud to tell.

Chapter Summary

- **Cultivating Connections:** Establish a supportive community that assists in navigating the creative

landscape. This network is essential for collaboration, sharing ideas, and mutual understanding.
- **Exchange of Expertise:** Sharing experiences is crucial, as it both enhances personal understanding and aids in the professional growth of others.
- **The Gift of Feedback:** Constructive criticism is invaluable. Establish a circle of trust for honest and productive feedback.
- **Consistency Over Perfection:** It's all about showing up regularly, trusting the creative process, and appreciating incremental progress.
- **Celebrating Progress:** Mark your milestones and often reflect on progress to maintain motivation and perspective.

Takeaways:

- Relationships are as crucial as skills in a creative career; find your tribe and foster those connections.
- Sharing knowledge is a two-way street that enriches everyone involved.
- Embrace constructive criticism for continual improvement.
- Prioritize consistent effort over elusive perfection to build a body of work.
- Acknowledge and celebrate your progress to appreciate the journey and fuel future endeavors.

6

WORKING WITH A TEAM

Until now, we've navigated the time management landscape solo. But the truth is, most of us play in a band – metaphorically speaking. When part of a team, syncing up our individual timings becomes crucial. It's one thing to manage our own schedule, quite another to harmonize it with others.

Achieving success isn't a one-person show; it's about collaboration. Recognizing that your team members have their own agendas, goals, and timelines is vital. It's about establishing a rhythm that works for everyone.

This chapter zooms into the collective aspect of time management. We're looking at how to align our individual time with the group's tempo without stepping on each other's toes. It's about coordination, cooperation, and sometimes, a little compromise. Let's break down the strategies that keep the whole band playing in synch.

TEAM BUILDING AND COLLABORATION

Effective time management is the backbone of any successful team, especially in creative endeavors where collaboration is vital. When a team synchronizes its schedules and objectives, it lays the groundwork for a harmonious and productive partnership.

Here's why it matters:

- **Shared Vision:** A clear idea of where you want to go aligns individual efforts with the team's collective goal, creating a unified direction for everyone involved.
- **Productive Workflow:** Efficiency maximizes productivity, minimizing stress and reducing the risk of burnout.
- **Balanced Contributions:** Ensures that workloads are fairly distributed, preventing any team member from becoming overwhelmed.
- **Open Communication:** Regular check-ins keep everyone informed about the project's progress and individual responsibilities.
- **Boosted Morale:** A team that works well together enjoys higher satisfaction as each member sees how their contributions fit into the larger picture.
- **Adaptability:** A good time management strategy includes the flexibility to accommodate creative sparks and unexpected changes without derailing

the project. This is essential when dealing with a group of creatives.

Managing a team's time in a creative setting isn't about strict schedules; it's about crafting a framework that supports everyone's best work, ensuring that all the pieces come together seamlessly.

Techniques for effective communication and delegation

Earlier we spoke about specific tools and techniques for personal time management, and you'll be happy to know that the tools for team communication and delegation are more a collection of skills than tangible items. The more conscious you are about these skills, the easier it will be to clearly put them into action. When you think about it, timing is essential in music, and a band director oversees, amongst all things, keeping rhythm. Let's look at some of these techniques and what they mean.

- **Clear Definition of Roles:** This involves explicitly outlining the responsibilities and expectations for each team member to prevent overlaps and ensure everyone understands their part in the project.
- **Consistent Check-Ins:** Regularly scheduled meetings to discuss progress, address issues, and

ensure alignment with the project's goals. These can vary from daily stand-ups to weekly reviews, depending on the project's needs.
- **Leveraging Digital Tools:** Utilizing project management software and tools to track tasks, deadlines, and progress. This approach enhances transparency and coordination among team members.
- **Autonomy Within the Team:** Empowering team members to make decisions within their areas of responsibility. This delegation fosters a sense of ownership and can lead to increased motivation and innovation.
- **Practicing Active Listening:** Engaging in attentive and empathetic listening during interactions with team members to fully understand their perspectives, ideas, and concerns.
- **Structured Delegation:** Assigning tasks and responsibilities clearly and logically, ensuring that team members have the necessary information and resources to complete them effectively.
- **Constructive Feedback:** Offering and encouraging feedback that is specific, actionable, and focused on improvement, thereby fostering a culture of continuous development.
- **Time Zone Sensitivity:** Being mindful of and accommodating different time zones when

scheduling meetings and setting deadlines, especially in globally distributed teams.
- **Meticulous Record-Keeping:** Maintaining comprehensive and accurate records of decisions, discussions, and task assignments to ensure clarity, continuity and accountability.
- **Recognition of Efforts:** Acknowledging and appreciating the hard work and achievements of team members, which can serve as a powerful motivator.

REAL-LIFE EXAMPLES OF SUCCESSFUL COLLABORATION IN THE MUSIC INDUSTRY

As we turn our attention back to Alex, she's in the critical stages of completing her project. It's a period were managing her time and aligning her team's efforts is more important than ever. Let's explore how Alex can apply some of these essential techniques to efficiently guide her project across the finish line.

CLEAR DEFINITION OF ROLES:

Alex assigns specific responsibilities: a mixing engineer for sound, a graphic artist for the album cover, and a marketing specialist for promotion. This ensures each team member knows their role.

Consistent Check-Ins:

She holds brief, regular meetings to track progress and address any concerns, keeping the team aligned and on schedule.

Leveraging Digital Tools:

Alex uses project management tools like Trello to monitor each aspect of the album, from production to marketing, keeping everyone updated.

Autonomy Within the Team:

She trusts her team members with decision-making power in their domains, fostering creativity and efficiency.

Active Listening:

In meetings, Alex makes sure to listen to her team's ideas and concerns, valuing their contributions and fostering a collaborative environment.

Delegation:

Alex delegates tasks clearly, such as social media management to her marketing specialist, providing clear outcomes but allowing them the freedom to execute.

Constructive Feedback:

She maintains an open feedback loop where constructive criticism is welcomed and used to make timely adjustments.

Time Zone Sensitivity:

Collaborating with a mastering engineer in a different time zone, Alex schedules meetings at convenient times and sets realistic deadlines.

Meticulous Record-Keeping:

Alex documents all decisions and discussions to ensure everyone is on the same page, even if they couldn't attend a meeting.

Recognition of Efforts:

When milestones are achieved, like finalizing a track, Alex acknowledges these achievements, boosting team morale and motivation.

How to Manage Team Members' Time Effectively

Managing a team's time effectively is a delicate balance, especially considering each member has their own life and commitments outside of your project. Recognizing and respecting this fact is crucial. It's like the difference between a well-rehearsed band and a spontaneous jam session - while both have their charm, in a professional setting, you want the precision and harmony of the former.

A clear, well-thought-out plan sets the stage. It's about laying out expectations for everyone's involvement -- when they need to step in and how much time they should allocate. This structured approach ensures that each team member can integrate their project responsibilities into their personal schedules without unnecessary stress or confusion.

Imagine calling a band member randomly at 1 AM for a session because you missed a beat earlier in the day. It's not just inconvenient; it's a recipe for frustration. Instead, scheduled rehearsals, where everyone knows in advance when they're needed, lead to better preparation and ultimately, a better performance.

- **Set Realistic Deadlines:** Understand each team member's capacity and other commitments. Set deadlines that are achievable, considering these factors.
- **Prioritize Tasks:** Not all tasks require immediate attention. Prioritize them based on urgency and importance, so team members know what to focus on first.
- **Flexible Scheduling:** Allow for some flexibility in schedules. Strict timings can be counterproductive, especially in creative processes.

- Use Time-Blocking: Allocate specific blocks of time for different project phases or tasks. This helps in organizing the team's workload more effectively.
- **Regular Updates:** Keep the team informed about project progress and any changes in scheduling or priorities. Transparency in communication is key.
- **Encourage Time Off:** Ensure team members take regular breaks and have time off. Overworking can lead to burnout and decreased productivity.
- **Respect Personal Time:** Avoid intruding on team members' personal time for project work, unless absolutely necessary.

By considering these aspects, you can manage your team's time in a way that's respectful of their individual needs while still keeping your project on track. It's about finding that sweet spot where everyone's time is valued and used efficiently.

7

OVERCOMING PROCRASTINATION AND DISTRACTIONS

Imagine this all-too-familiar scenario: You're charged up, ready to seize control of your time. You sit down, craft the perfect plan, outline an ideal project, even sketch out a top-notch workout and diet routine. But then, reality hits. When it's time to put your plan into action, that initial surge of motivation and drive begins to wane. It reminds me of what one of my mentors used to say: "Motivation is bullshit." What he meant was, true value in executing a plan lies in doing it whether you 'feel like it' or not. It's about discipline, not just desire.

For us creatives, our work often springs from a 'vibe' or a 'feeling.' We ride the waves of inspiration. However, it's crucial to harness these waves intentionally. Your mindset and attitude aren't just part of the process; they're the cornerstone of it. They determine how effectively you overcome distractions and stick to your plan. Let's dive into how a disciplined mindset can be a game-changer in managing time, especially when creativity is at the heart of what you do.

Mindset and Attitude

For creatives, self-discipline means showing up at the canvas, the studio, or the keyboard, regardless of how inspired you are at the moment. This commitment is what differentiates the hobbyist from the professional. Here are a few things to always keep in the forefront.

Growth Mindset vs. Fixed Mindset

Embrace a growth mindset where you see your talents and abilities as evolving qualities as opposed to a fixed trait. This perspective helps you remain open to learning and improvement, turning challenges into opportunities to expand your creative horizons.

Mindfulness and Presence

In a world full of distractions, being present in your creative process is a superpower. Mindfulness helps you focus, pushing away the noise and bringing clarity to your work. It's about immersing yourself fully in the task at hand, whether it's writing a lyric or composing a melody. This presence can elevate the quality of your work exponentially.

MANAGING EXPECTATIONS

Setting realistic expectations is key to avoiding unnecessary frustration. It's understanding that creativity isn't always about grand eureka moments; sometimes, it's a slow, steady grind. By managing your expectations, you allow yourself to embrace the small victories and progress, no matter how incremental.

EMBRACING THE PROCESS

The real joy in creativity often lies in the process, not just the outcome. It's about finding fulfillment in the act of creation itself — the trials, the errors, the moments of flow. This approach balances your drive for results with a recognition of the value inherent in the creative journey.

CULTIVATING PATIENCE AND PERSEVERANCE

Patience and perseverance are your allies in the long haul of your creative career. They remind you that some projects take time to mature, and that endurance is often as important as raw talent. In the dance of creativity, these qualities keep you moving to the rhythm of your long-term vision, even when the steps get complicated.

ATTITUDE TOWARDS FAILURE

How you respond to setbacks can either stall or propel your creative journey. See failure not as a defeat but as a necessary part of your growth – an indispensable teacher that paves the way for future successes. In short, be kind to yourself.

OVERCOMING PROCRASTINATION AND DISTRACTIONS

There is no greater challenge you will face as a creator managing your time than procrastination and distractions. Creative work relies heavily on focus and discipline, but sometimes it's easy to wander off the path. In the realm of creativity, where ideas and inspiration flow freely, it can be all too tempting to drift into daydreams or get sidetracked by less demanding things.

Breaking the Procrastination Cycle

Procrastination often stems from feeling overwhelmed or fearing failure. To break this cycle, start by simplifying tasks. Divide larger projects into smaller, more manageable chunks. This makes starting less daunting and progress more tangible. Remember, every small step forward counts.

Setting up a dedicated workspace can also create a mental boundary between work and leisure. This physical distinction helps signal to your brain that it's time to focus. Make this space inviting and beneficial to your creative process – a place where you feel motivated and undisturbed.

HANDLING DISTRACTIONS

Distractions, especially in this digital age, are a constant battle. The key is to set clear boundaries. Like mentioned earlier in the book, allocate specific times for checking emails, social media, or other potential distractions, and stick to them. Consider using apps that limit your access to distracting websites during work hours.

Mindfulness practices can be incredibly beneficial in enhancing concentration. Techniques like meditation help train your mind to stay present and resist the urge to wander. Even a few minutes of mindfulness each day can make a significant difference in your ability to focus.

TIME BLOCKING FOR CREATIVE WORK

Time blocking can be a powerful tool for creatives. Allocate blocks of time for specific tasks and commit to working only on those tasks during those periods. This method helps in minimizing multitasking, which can dilute your focus and effectiveness.

Remember, dealing with procrastination and distractions is not about perfection; it's about progress. It's about finding and refining strategies that work for you, allowing you to stay on track and make the most of your creative time. By acknowledging these challenges and actively working to overcome them, you can transform your approach to time management and elevate your creative output.

MINDFULNESS AND SELF-AWARENESS

It seems that terms like 'mindfulness' and 'self-awareness' are often tossed around, but let's take a moment to really understand what they mean and why they're so crucial for anyone striving to master time management. Mindfulness, in its essence, is about being fully present in the moment. It's the art of paying attention to your current experience without judgment or distraction. For creatives, this means immersing yourself wholly in the creative task at hand, whether it's writing a song, painting a canvas, or brainstorming ideas for a new project. It's about silencing the noise of the outside world to listen to the rhythm of your thoughts and the flow of your creativity.

Practicing mindfulness can be tricky, the truth is, a lot of us are not comfortable being alone with our thoughts, so we constantly seek distractions to keep our minds from speaking to us. But for creatives, mindfulness is more than just a practice; it's a way of enhancing the very essence of our creativity. At its core, it's about being intensely aware of what you are sensing and feeling at the moment, without interpretation or judgement. In my personal experience being mindful is a great way to combat creative blocks. These blocks are often the result of overthinking or mental clutter. Mindfulness clears your mental space, placing you in a better position to receive fresh ideas and clear perspectives. Here's a few things you can do to start implementing mindfulness into your day:

Rise

Start your day by acknowledging your existence. It can be as simple as spending five minutes in silence, focusing on your breath, or doing a short, guided meditation. Wiggle your fingers, feel your hair, listen to the silence. This sets a calm, centered tone for the day.

Observe

Dedicate a few minutes each day to observe your surroundings with full attention. It could be focusing on a piece of art, watching the leaves rustle in the wind, or simply observing the people around you. Notice the details, colors, sounds, and textures.

Write

Take a few moments each day to jot down what's on your mind. This simple act of writing can be incredibly powerful in decluttering your thoughts. It's like having a casual chat with yourself, where you lay out what you're feeling and thinking. This process can be a wellspring of creativity, as it often uncovers hidden insights and sparks new ideas. Remember, journaling doesn't need to be an elaborate exercise. It can be as straightforward as pulling out your phone, opening the notes app, and typing out a simple sentence like "Today was a good day." You'll be surprised at how often that single line leads to a cascade of thoughts waiting to be expressed.

LISTEN

When you're listening to music, give it your full attention – just immerse yourself in the sound and nothing else. Pay close attention to the intricate details – the distinct instruments, the rhythm's ebb and flow, the story told by the lyrics. This focused listening does more than just deepen your appreciation of the music; it hones your ability to pick up on the finer details in complex compositions. More importantly, it sharpens your listening skills – an essential tool in any creative professional's kit.

MOVE

If you're feeling stuck creatively, take a walk. Focus on the sensation of your feet touching the ground, the rhythm of your steps, and the sights and sounds around you. This can be a great way to clear your head and find new inspiration.

BREATHE

Practice mindful breathing throughout the day. Focus on your breath, notice the inhale and exhale, and try to make them deep and even. This can be done almost anywhere and is an excellent way to center yourself when you feel overwhelmed or scattered.

Disconnect

Take short breaks during your day. It could be focusing on a cup of coffee as you drink it, doing a quick body scan to relax any tension, or simply sitting quietly and noticing your thoughts without judgment.

Create

Engage in your art mindfully, be it playing an instrument, painting, or writing. Pay attention to every detail of the process, immerse yourself in the act, and let go of concerns about the outcome.

Self-awareness, on the other hand, is the conscious knowledge of one's own character, feelings, motives, and desires. It's like having an internal mirror that reflects your true self, helping you understand why you react the way you do, what triggers your procrastination, what times of day your energy peaks, and what environments stimulate your creativity. This self-knowledge is invaluable in managing your time effectively, as it guides you to make choices that align with your personal rhythms and creative inclinations.

Remember, there's a fine line between having confidence in your skills and talents and the humble realization that growth and learning never cease. Striking this balance is crucial, influencing not only what you create but also your personal evolution and sense of fulfillment. To help you cultivate greater self-awareness, here are some techniques that have been effective in my own experience:

UNDERSTAND YOUR CREATIVE CYCLE

Each creative has a cycle – times when you're overflowing with ideas and energy, and times when the well seems dry. Self-awareness helps you recognize these patterns. By understanding your cycle, you can better plan your schedule, aligning demanding creative tasks with your high-energy phases and saving more routine tasks for your low-energy moments.

IDENTIFY TRIGGERS AND DISTRACTIONS

Self-awareness enables you to identify what triggers your procrastination or what distracts you most. Is it social media, a cluttered workspace, or perhaps emotional stress? Recognizing these triggers is the first step in creating strategies to overcome them and stay focused on your creative goals. When you catch yourself straying from your intended task, take a moment to reflect. Ask yourself what pulled you away from your work. Understanding this can be a revealing exercise in staying aligned with your creative pursuits.

LEVERAGE STRENGTHS AND ACKNOWLEDGE WEAKNESSES

It's important to recognize not just what you're good at, but also where you might need help or improvement. This understanding allows you to leverage your strengths to their fullest while seeking support or development in areas where you're less confident.

Balance Ambition with Well-being

Being deeply passionate about what you do can often lead to a sense of needing to be constantly engaged, but it's crucial to find a balance between your ambition and your personal well-being. Recognize that overextending yourself will eventually result in burnout. Sometimes, the most productive thing you can do is to give yourself permission to step back and recharge. We'll explore this concept further in the upcoming chapter.

Feedback and Growth

Be open to feedback, using it as a tool for growth and improvement. This openness is crucial for personal and professional development, allowing you to continuously evolve and adapt in your creative journey.

Be Confident and Continually Learn

Being confident in your skills and who you are is a vital part of a creative's self-awareness. It fuels your ability to present your work with conviction and to take on challenges with a positive attitude. However, this confidence must be coupled with the understanding that creativity is a lifelong journey of learning. Every project, every collaboration, and every challenge are an opportunity to learn something new, to refine your skills, and to expand your creative horizons.

BE KIND AND PATIENT WITH YOURSELF

Equally important in the realm of self-awareness is being kind and patient with yourself. Creativity doesn't adhere to a strict timeline or a linear path. There will be moments of exceptional breakthroughs as well as periods of stagnation. Recognizing and accepting this ebb and flow without harsh self-judgment is crucial. It's about giving yourself the space to grow at your own pace, understanding that each step – whether forward or seemingly backward – is part of your unique journey.

Chapter 7 Summary

Alright, let's recap what we've tackled in this chapter. It's all about the mind games we play with ourselves when it comes to time management, especially for us creatives.

- **Mindset Matters:** First things first, your mindset is key. It's about pushing through even when you're not feeling 100% inspired. It's truly what separates the pros from the hobbyists.
- **Beating Procrastination and Distractions:** We all get sidetracked or hit the procrastination wall. We talked about some solid ways to stay on track and keep your eyes on the prize.
- **The Mindful Creative:** Mindfulness and being aware of what's going on inside your head can really amp up your focus and creativity. We went over some practical ways to bring mindfulness into your everyday routine.
- **Confidence vs. Constant Learning:** It's important to be confident in your skills, but remember, there's always room to grow. And hey, be easy on yourself – ups and downs are part of the creative process.

8

THE POWER OF INTENTIONAL LIVING

As I mentioned at the start of this book, my early days in the music industry were a rollercoaster of relentless work periods followed by stretches of complete inactivity. Back then, my personal life took a back seat – catching up with friends, hitting the gym, or even just calling family members wasn't on my radar. When I began to get a handle on managing my time, my initial focus was purely professional. I had a meticulously planned calendar and a forward-looking plan, something I hadn't considered before. However, I soon realized a crucial piece was missing – the balance with my personal life.

Time management, as it turns out, isn't a skill reserved for our professional endeavors. It's equally vital in our personal lives. In fact, they're inseparably linked – you can't truly succeed in one without the other.

The pursuit of work-life balance is admittedly challenging, particularly in a culture that glorifies constant busyness as a measure of productivity. I question this hustle mentality. Taking time to reflect, to be with loved ones, and to indulge in activities that rejuvenate you isn't just leisure; it's an essential part of fueling your drive for success. What's the value of wealth and success if you have no one to share it with or no time to enjoy it in your best years?

Intentionality is the cornerstone here. Whatever you choose to do, do it with purpose. We'll explore how to practice intentional living later in this chapter. But first, let's understand why being intentional matters and how setting clear priorities lays the groundwork for achieving this balance.

INTENTIONAL LIVING AND SETTING PRIORITIES

My journey to achieving a work-life balance that I was comfortable took a significant turn when I began to intentionally allocate time for my personal priorities. It started with something as simple as committing my lunch hour at 1 PM every day. This small act set a rhythm to my day, making this time slot sacred yet sometimes flexible. But it wasn't just about scheduling meals. I began dedicating time to the things that got lost in the daily grind – like phoning my mom, planning dates with my significant other, and even immersing myself in a good book. This shift didn't just reorganize my schedule; it felt like I was unlocking more hours in my day. I suddenly had more time to complete my work and do the things I enjoy.

However, this transformation wasn't an overnight thing. It began with a heart-to-heart with myself. I dug deep to uncover my real values. What brings me joy? What gives me a sense of fulfillment? It was important that I wrote them down, turning them into tangible guides for my everyday choices. Now, when faced with tough decisions, I first check in with these values. Does this align with what's truly important to me?

Here's how it works: Your priorities should be a clear mirror of your values. Then, your goals naturally align with these priorities. Take my case – I value being healthy. So, I set my priorities around maintaining a healthy diet and regular exercise. My goals then became specific: cooking at home at least five times a week and hitting the gym four times a week. With these goals in mind, I intentionally block out time in my calendar for them. For instance, I make sure to set aside gym time early in the morning and protect my lunch hour for healthy eating and meal prep. This strategy ensures that less important tasks don't disrupt these key activities.

So, the takeaway here is simple yet profound: Start by figuring out what you truly value. These values are the bedrock upon which you build your priorities and, subsequently, your goals. It's a strategy that brings clarity and direction, helping you navigate both your personal and professional life with purpose.

STRATEGIES FOR AVOIDING BURNOUT

Growing up, I was surrounded by the hustle culture. Hard work and long hours were touted as the golden tickets to success. Taking a break? That was often labeled as laziness or a lack of dedication. But something about this didn't sit right with me. Was life meant to be an endless grind during our best years, only to find ourselves too drained to enjoy the fruits of our labor later? Surely, there had to be a better way – a balance between the relentless push and the equally important joys of life.

Life is more than just our careers. It's about those experiences that enrich us, the moments of relaxation that rejuvenate us, and the joy we find in being with loved ones, engaging in passions outside of work.

Now, there's no shortage of literature on striking the perfect work-life balance. Here, I want to share the strategies that have personally worked for me, along with some insights into their potential downsides. Because let's face it – no approach is perfect, and what works for one might not work for another. It's all about finding your unique equilibrium.

Recognize Burnout

The first step in combating burnout is recognizing its signs and understanding how it affects you personally. For me, burnout manifests as brain fog, heavy eyes, and an elusive creative zone – it's like hitting a wall where inspiration and energy should be. But here's a crucial point: don't mix up burnout with simple procrastination. It's vital to be honest with yourself in these moments. Are you truly burnt out, or just facing a distraction? Learning to distinguish between these two can guide you toward the right approach. Some strategies work best as preventative measures, while others are more about reacting and coping when burnout hits.

<u>Establish Clear Boundaries</u>

Navigating the balance between work and personal life is challenging, yet essential. Whether you're self-employed or part of a larger organization, drawing a line between professional responsibilities and personal time is crucial. Just as it's important to keep personal distractions out of work hours (like saving that catch-up call with your friend for post-work hours), it's equally vital not to let work tasks spill over into your personal life.

Commit to your work hours, whether that's 8, 10, or however many hours suit your rhythm. Stick to them diligently, then make your best effort to just stop. If you find yourself struggling to be productive in those hours, it's often a signal of underlying issues – maybe it's a lack of planning or unclear priorities. If that's the case, addressing the root cause is key. Are you spreading yourself too thin?

But there's a flip side. Working with others, especially when dealing with different time zones or night owls, requires some flexibility. It's about setting boundaries while being adaptable. Perhaps you start your day later to sync with international team members or accommodate those who hit their stride at night. The goal is to be deliberate with your time while remaining agile in its allocation. As discussed earlier, time blocking is an invaluable tool here, helping you manage your hours effectively while staying open to necessary adjustments.

Stay Organized

At the heart of preventing burnout lies a simple yet powerful tool: staying organized. It boils down to two classic instruments - your calendar and your journal. These aren't just accessories; they're the twin engines that drive your daily life.

Let's talk about your calendar. It's more than a collection of dates and appointments; it's your timekeeper. By setting deadlines and scheduling tasks, you spread out your workload. It's like having a built-in promise that there's time set aside tomorrow for what you can't finish today. No more frantic scrambling to get everything done at once.

Then, there's journaling. This isn't just about penning down your thoughts; it's about giving them a place to live outside your head. When your thoughts are down on paper, they become more manageable. They're no longer swirling around in your mind, causing distraction and unease. Have a task you keep thinking about? Schedule it. Someone you need to call? Add it to the calendar. Struggling with a decision? Write it out, read it back, and watch as clarity emerges from the chaos of doubt.

By integrating these tools into your routine, you're not just organizing your days; you're streamlining your entire process of thinking and doing. It's about bringing order to the mental and the physical, ensuring that everything has its place and time.

Delegate

Delegation isn't just a business term; it's an essential strategy for any creative looking to maximize their time and focus on what truly matters. At its core, delegation is about entrusting tasks to others, freeing up your space to concentrate on your main priorities.

We often associate delegation with a workplace setting, where a manager assigns tasks to team members to optimize productivity and maintain focus on the broader goals. For creatives, it works similarly. By delegating routine or specialized tasks, you open more room in your schedule for those high-priority, creative endeavors. Take my example: despite having a background in audio engineering, I choose to delegate the mixing process of my records. Why? Because the 4-6 hours spent mixing could be better utilized in crafting new music.

Delegation extends into our personal lives as well, often more than we realize. Hiring someone to mow your lawn, for instance, buys you an extra hour or two, which can then be invested in something more significant or fulfilling.

The essence of effective delegation lies in being intentional about what tasks you pass on. It's less about shrugging off what you don't want to do and more about evaluating whether a task is the best use of your time, considering all your priorities. Remember, every act of delegation should be a strategic decision, rooted in the pursuit of your goals and the efficient use of your time.

REGULAR BREAKS AND VACATIONS

This isn't the first time in this book I'm mentioning the importance of breaks, but it's a point worth driving home: regular breaks are essential. Studies back this up, showing that our brains function best when we balance intense focus with periods of rest. Think of it like a dance of give and take. For every intense work session (the giving part), there should be a moment to step back, to breathe, and to recharge (the taking part). Maybe it's stepping away from your computer every half hour or so to grab some water – and remember, drink that water away from your desk. It's about more than just hydration; it's a mini reset for your mind.

And then, there's the big one: vacations. It's crucial to carve out substantial time away from work at least once a year. Planning is key here. Pick a time that allows you to genuinely disconnect, ensuring there are no looming deadlines or major projects that could intrude on your relaxation. Delegate tasks that can be handled in your absence. I remember having an album mastered while I was off enjoying a vacation. It was seamless – I came back, gave it a thumbs up, and moved it along for distribution. Had I waited until after my holiday to tackle this, I would've lost a week of work and, worse, spent my vacation time dwelling on unfinished business. So, plan your brief pauses and your extended getaways with the same level of intention. Your mind, body, and creativity will thank you for it.

Prioritize Self-Care

Self-care is a buzzword these days, with countless articles and books singing its praises. But what does it really mean? It's about taking proactive steps to maintain your well-being and happiness, especially under stress. Think of it as a form of ritual, much like the daily routines we do without a second thought, such as brushing our teeth or attending weekly worship services. The goal here is to gradually incorporate practices into your life that actively contribute to your well-being. Let's break it down:

- **Regular Exercise:** It's not about becoming a fitness fanatic. Something as simple as a 30-minute walk after lunch or work can make a world of difference, provided it's done consistently. Remember, consistency is key – schedule it in your calendar to make it a part of your routine.
- **Hobbies:** Ever wanted to start a new hobby? Whether it's baking, knitting, or even gaming, the key is to allocate specific time slots for these activities. Enjoy your gaming session, but when the timer goes off, it's time to wrap it up.
- **Meditation:** You don't need to be an expert to meditate. Start by spending five minutes in quiet contemplation, listening to your thoughts without engaging or acting on them. It's a chance to slow down and tune in to what's going on in your mind.
- **Intentional Rest:** This might sound trivial, but take a nap, go for a walk, or listen to music for 20 minutes. The trick is to do these things deliberately and within a set time frame.

Seek your Support System

Sometimes, the most effective way to deal with burnout is to reach out to trusted individuals or those who have faced similar challenges. Having a network of support can be crucial in guiding you through tough times.

Every successful person I've encountered has had mentors. It's nearly impossible to navigate the complexities of life and career without guidance from those who have already walked the path. Besides mentors, having a group of peers in similar fields can be invaluable. For instance, I have a group of creative friends with whom I regularly exchange ideas, support, and motivation. This isn't just about professional networking; it's a mutual exchange of support that spans both our professional and personal lives.

Finding a mentor can seem daunting, but it's about taking that first step. When I was 16 and aspiring to be a record producer in a pre-social media world, I reached out to a producer whose work I admired and told him straight up, "I want to do what you do." Maybe it was luck, maybe audacity, but it was certainly It was a bold move that led to a lifelong mentorship that is still a cornerstone in my life today. Now, with platforms like LinkedIn and Instagram, connecting with potential mentors has become more accessible. The key is to approach them sincerely and respectfully, understanding the value of their time and experience. Remember, it's about building a relationship, not just seeking advice.

Reflect and Adjust

Regularly stepping back for a self-audit can be a powerful tool in preventing burnout. It's about introspection, understanding the root causes, and adjusting accordingly. If you find yourself struggling with mental fatigue or a lack of inspiration, it's time to ask some critical questions. Am I overcommitting? Are my goals realistic? Could I break my tasks into more manageable pieces? Writing down these thoughts can shift them from overwhelming internal noise to clear, actionable items on paper. This shift in perspective is often all it takes to start making effective changes.

Utilizing your available resources, such as meditation techniques or your carefully planned calendar, can be instrumental in these adjustments. Consistent, mindful adjustments can keep burnout at bay.

Moreover, incorporating a nightly journaling routine provides a space for reflection on your day. Did you feel in control, energized, and fulfilled with your activities? This simple act of self-inquiry can uncover patterns that might lead to burnout, allowing you to make subtle yet impactful changes to your routine before any real burnout sets in.

Celebrate

A good friend of mine and fellow creative once told me, "Bro, don't forget to put both feet on the step before climbing to the next one." This advice resonated deeply with me. I was always so focused on reaching the next goal that I seldom paused to appreciate the milestones I had achieved.

It's crucial to celebrate your victories, no matter their size. A round of drinks with your band after a grueling recording session, a special dinner for consistently hitting the gym all month, or even hanging a plaque for your first million Spotify streams - these acts of celebration are essential. They're more than just rewards; they're acknowledgments and affirmations of your journey and growth. Celebrating your achievements, big and small, is vital. It keeps you motivated and energized, offering positive reinforcement that you're staying true to your plan and continually evolving. After all, if you don't take the time to celebrate your own successes, who else will?

As these practices become a part of your daily life, they evolve into habits, as natural as brushing your teeth. The trick is to stick with it, be adaptable, and be gentle with yourself. Missed a day? Understand why, but don't beat yourself up. Remember, the ultimate goal is your personal growth and becoming the best version of yourself.

HOW TO CREATE A FULFILLING AND BALANCED LIFE

A balanced life is less about reaching a perfect state and more about navigating the dynamic flow of our daily experiences. This journey is deeply personal and varies for each individual. For some, fulfillment might mean immersing in the hustle and bustle of a busy career, while for others, it's found in quieter moments. The key is understanding that life's balance is not static; it's an ongoing process of adjustment and realignment.

Finding Your Unique Balance:

Creating a fulfilling and balanced life is an art that involves navigating the dynamic ebb and flow of our daily experiences. It's a deeply personal journey, unique to everyone. For some, fulfillment might be found in the hustle and bustle of a busy career, while others may find it in the tranquility of quieter moments. The essence of achieving this balance lies in understanding that it's not about reaching a perfect state, but rather about continually adjusting and realigning as life unfolds.

In my journey, I've realized that the balance I sought was not a fixed destination, but a fluid, ever-changing state. It's about being in tune with your own needs and desires and recognizing that these can shift and evolve over time. The true equilibrium comes from being adaptable and responsive to these changes.

Here are four practical tips for creating a balanced life:

- **Embrace the Journey:** Understand that seeking balance is an evolving process. It involves learning from both achievements and setbacks.
- **Celebrate your successes**, but also be open to learning from the times when things don't go as planned.

- **Diversity in Balance:** Acknowledge that balance looks different at various life stages. What works for you today might change tomorrow, and that's perfectly fine. Stay adaptable and open to new routines and approaches.
- **Joy vs. Happiness:** Distinguish between external joy and internal happiness. While external achievements and relationships can bring joy, true happiness is an internal state, often achieved through self-awareness and contentment with your life's journey.

In my own life, I've found that balance is not about dividing my time equally between work and leisure, but about finding harmony between the two. It's about knowing when to push forward and when to step back and recharge. There have been plenty of times where my harmony was found in long, uninterrupted recording sessions, or a week of working late every day.

Ultimately, a fulfilling life is about making intentional choices that resonate with who you are and what you value. It's about understanding that balance is not a fixed target, but a fluid, ongoing journey that requires continuous effort and adjustment.

Conclusion

As we reach the final pages of this book, let's take a moment to reflect on the ground we've covered. From the outset, it became clear that time is our most precious currency, and mastering its intentional use is crucial for professional success and personal fulfillment. We've challenged the stereotype that creatives are inherently disorganized, uncovering ways to enhance creativity through effective time management. We've navigated common challenges, taking cues from Alex's successful project release, and covered everything from setting goals to the delicate dance of collaboration. Each chapter has been a step towards understanding and embracing time management as an essential aspect of our creative existence. This journey was about making every hour meaningful and balanced across our creative, professional, and personal lives.

In my own life, practicing time management has been transformative. The moments of significant success, clarity, and fulfillment coincided with taking control of my time. I've learned to identify and prioritize what's truly valuable, acknowledging that values evolve with experiences. This book is a testament that we don't have to resign ourselves to the idea that 'creatives are just disorganized.' It's a myth we're well equipped to dispel, and I hope this book serves as a guide to help you harness your time, embrace your creativity, and live a life that resonates with your most authentic self.

Remember, the theories and strategies we've explored are most powerful when put into consistent practice. The cornerstone of mastering time is your mindset. When jotting down your values, ensure that time sits at the top. It's also essential to recognize that these strategies aren't a one-size-fits-all solution. Being conscious of what resonates with you and what doesn't is crucial in shaping your unique approach to time management.

Moreover, mastering time management is an ongoing journey, not a one-time transformation. It demands continuous learning, adaptation, and refinement. Time is your most valuable asset; treating it with the importance it deserves is imperative. This book is woven from my personal experiences and explorations in time management. I've shared techniques that have worked for me and others that were challenging. However, the world of time management is vast and varied. There are numerous resources covering its scientific and psychological aspects. I encourage you to continue exploring to gain diverse perspectives and deeper insights. Embrace this

CONCLUSION

journey of learning and adaptation and watch as time transforms from a scarce commodity into a powerful ally in your creative endeavors.

Author Bio

sP Polanco is a renowned music producer, songwriter, and industry consultant with over two decades of experience. Based in New York City and Miami, Polanco has worked with top Latin artists, earning four Latin Grammy nominations. His expertise spans across genres, with a notable impact in modernizing and globalizing bachata. As a former Director of Artist Relations & Strategy at Warner Music Latina, Polanco played a pivotal role in shaping artist careers. Now leading SP Music, he continues to innovate, mentoring emerging talent and expanding the reach of Latin music globally.

Made in the USA
Columbia, SC
06 November 2024